D0966549

*We all have a homosexual who is asleep.
There are some who wake up, others who do
not. This could happen to everyone. It takes the
right place, with the right moment, with the
right person.*

—Victoria Abril, The French Twist

No Previous Experience

a memoir of love and change

Elspeth Cameron

VIKING

VIKING
Published by the Penguin Group
Penguin Books Canada Ltd, 10 Alcorn Avenue, Toronto, Ontario, Canada
M4V 3B2
Penguin Books Ltd, 27 Wrights Lane, London W8 5TZ, England
Viking Penguin, a division of Penguin Books USA Inc., 375 Hudson Street,
New York, New York 10014, U.S.A.
Penguin Books Australia Ltd, Ringwood, Victoria, Australia
Penguin Books (NZ) Ltd, cnr Rosedale and Airborne Roads,
Albany, Auckland 1310, New Zealand

Penguin Books Ltd, Registered Offices: Harmondsworth,
Middlesex, England

First published 1997

1 3 5 7 9 10 8 6 4 2
Copyright © Elspeth Cameron, 1997

Printed and bound in Canada on acid free paper ∞

Canadian Cataloguing in Publication Data

Cameron, Elspeth, 1943–
No previous experience: a memoir of love and change

ISBN 0-670-87376-4

1. Cameron, Elspeth, 1943–. 2. Lesbians – Canada – Biography.
3. Biographers – Canada – Biography. 4. Lesbian couples – Canada –
Biography. I. Title.

HQ75.4.C35A3 1997   306.76'63'092   C96-932086-8

Visit Penguin Canada's web site at **www.penguin.ca**

To J.

Forever and Ever

E.

Acknowledgments

This book could not have happened without the support of the Social Sciences and Humanities Federation of Canada. I also thank Ged Martin, Director of the Centre of Canadian Studies, University of Edinburgh, and Rae Fleming, Visiting Fellow, University of Edinburgh, 1991.

The epigraph in this book is taken from an interview by Susan Fox Rogers with Victoria Abril about her role in the film *Gazon Maudit* (*The French Twist*) in *Curve* Magazine (Jan/Feb 1996). Excerpts from *Anne of Green Gables* are used with the authorization of the heirs of L. M. Montgomery. "Anne of Green Gables" is a trademark and Canadian official mark of the Anne of Green Gables Licensing Authority Inc., which is owned by the heirs of L. M. Montgomery and the Province of Prince Edward Island and located in Charlottetown, Prince Edward Island.

Many people have helped me, advertently or inadvertently, with this book. I wish especially to thank Gale Bildfell for her insight and support, and Susan Lawson for her suggestions. Meg Masters, Len Glickman, Catherine Marjoribanks and Cynthia Good have been wonderful to work with. Also, I am grateful in various ways to Lexie Cameron, Bea Buitenhuis, Hugo Cameron, Henry Lovejoy, John and Gail Pearce, David, Leopold and Anatol McGinnis, Susan Lamb, Leslie and Bev Chapin, Bill Stauble, Beth Balshaw, Lynn Sloane, Tammy Hallquist, Willie Johnson, Grace MacLean, Betty MacDonald and Gaile McGregor.

There are not words to express my appreciation to Janice Dickin.

NO PREVIOUS EXPERIENCE

One

IT CAN HAPPEN on a hike. You round a woody corner and suddenly you're in the clear on the brink of a pale limestone bluff, your stomach clenched, breath held, as you stare straight down into the lush damp valley you never suspected was there. Or you pass through the quiet streets of a nondescript town and a double rainbow arches right in front of you, so close you can see the iridescent droplets suspended midair, and you are speechless with wonder.

They used to tell it in books. A ride on a magic carpet through the midnight blue of Arabian nights. Looking down, you could glimpse exotic splendours: turbaned thieves, the flash of scimitars, mysterious minarets. You knew there was another reality behind closed doors in strange places. It was scary. You needed a password. Open Sesame.

I dimly recall an old movie. Was it Shangri-La? A lost plane? A Tibetan trek high into desolate snowdeep mountains? And all at once through a narrow wind-struck pass, with the suddenness of a blow on the face, there it was: a green valley, pastoral peace, a village of incomparable beauty, spread splendid in the sun.

Later I recognized it with an upwards rush of the hair on my neck. I knew without being told what stout Cortez, with his eagle eye, felt as he stood, silent, upon his peak in Darien.

It can happen when you aren't paying attention. You can miss the whole thing. You can be blinded by blizzards, forget the password, pass by the cliff or plunge to disaster over its edge.

It can happen anytime, anywhere.

Two

I DON'T REMEMBER meeting her.

She looms up into my memory suddenly, like a steep path on a hiking trail, at the reception after the conference. Mine had been the last paper, "Truth in Biography." I had relied on notes scribbled on the plane, staying up all night high over the Atlantic and arriving, harried, at the Canadian Studies Centre in Edinburgh just in time to deliver it. I'd written two biographies, had a third underway, and the main point in my paper was that there was no such thing as biographical truth. There were facts. There were situations. These could be documented. But there was another kind of truth, elusive, elastic, tantalizing, that I had tried, with only intermittent success, to realize.

The questions had been difficult. I had, after all, confessed that this biographer — like the Emperor — was wearing no clothes, had no truth to tell. And why had I never written about a woman? It was the question I always got. I didn't know why. I fudged as usual.

The reception was jammed with biographers, literary theorists, Canadianists, students — the usual flotsam of academic conferences. Deals were being made. One-upmanship was being played. Territory was being staked. Food was being consumed. Wine was being drunk. Especially by me.

I had just had an intense conversation with a theorist from my own university. She had peered at me from under a bush of violent red hair and informed me that if I did not eat something, I would put myself at risk of heart trouble. She knew. Her mother was a doctor. She had been observing me. I was too thin, a little flushed, drinking too much, eating nothing — after sleeplessness and the adrenaline rush of giving a paper. I turned away.

And there she was.

She was a biographer too. She had a dizzying name, something triple-barrelled. Her paper, given the day before I arrived, had a bewildering title: "Aimee Semple McPherson: Fantasizing the Fantasizer? Telling the Tale of a Tale-Teller." It was so incomprehensible I guessed she must be a postmodernist. All I could think of to say, still smarting from the lecture on the possibility of endangering my heart, was: "How odd! My subject, Earle Birney, once wrote a poem about your subject!"

I expected the eagerness of the magpie scholar. But she slowly drawled her response, "Oh, yeah. Men were always writing about Aimee. It means fuck-all."

I bubbled on, the verbal waterfall unleashed in my talk had been artificially dammed by strict time limits. And my tongue had now been loosened with relief and wine.

"But *this* poem is really interesting. He makes all these clever sexual and religious puns about her. He calls it 'Mammorial Stunzas for Aimee Simple McFarcin.'" I giggled. "It's quite clever. Do you want me to send you a copy?"

She didn't.

I went to get my coat in the hall a few minutes later. And there she was, one of a group of women headed for a play on Norman Bethune. "Can I join you?" I asked.

"Sure," said one of them, not her. I had already forgotten her triple-barrelled name.

This suited me. The play, then dinner with women. Before leaving Toronto behind me, I had made a single pledge to myself: do not be alone with a man. Slim, blond and highly skilled in concealing my intelligence from others, I had too often been a target. An invitation, she would say later. The Thinking Man's Barbie Doll. I had deliberately dressed like this since my teens. I had been desperate then to look feminine. Tall, flat-chested and wiry, I had earned the nickname "The Telephone Pole" on the basketball court. I was team captain and I could score forty-four points in a game, but all I really wanted was to look like the cheerleaders in their tight yellow sweaters and little green plaid kilts. To make matters worse, I was a brain. Boys — the only passport to social life — dreaded me. I dreaded social isolation. I wanted breasts, hips, blond hair, small feet, and I went about having them. I padded my bras with foam rubber, stuffed my hips with folded underpants, bleached my hair with Javex and crammed my feet into pointed pumps a size too small. Shaping my appearance to the desires of men became a habit. Shaping my behaviour to their needs had followed lock-step.

This was one of the first conferences I had dared attend alone over fourteen years of my marriage. Paul often came with me. He went to conferences all the time — two or three a year —

and he figured he knew what might happen to his wife on her own at a conference. I took my taupe houndstooth suit, the one I'd had made by Paul's tailor so I could look professional while teaching. Men wouldn't like it at all. I'd show him I could be trusted.

"Are any of you staying on tomorrow?" I asked as I left the dinner table later with one of the women whose bed-and-breakfast was near mine. No one responded. Undaunted, I pressed on. "Because if any of you are, I'd love company for dinner. I'm here for a week because I'm giving another paper at a different conference before I fly back. Anyway, you can find me at Thrum's."

I woke next morning to the unexpected joy of bright sunshine in Edinburgh. All day I walked — up to the Castle, across the bridge into Princes Street, over the wide heath south of Arthur's Seat and down to the Sheep's Heid pub in Duddingston, where I downed a pint of rich brown bitter and a ploughman's lunch in a cramped bright courtyard next to a flowery fountain. All day I faced into the sun, as if I could leave the shadows behind me.

On my return there was a message with a phone number under my door. "Janice Dickin McGinnis rang."

I called the number. Had I meant it about dinner? Okay, she'd come by Thrum's at seven o'clock.

I had already had three scotches at Bell's, the closest pub, before she met me at my overdecorated, overfurnished, overheated ground-floor room that gave onto a boxy flower garden.

I was pleased. I could keep my promise and enjoy it. Money, age and experience were enough to ensure social life. Men were redundant. I was happy, too, with the artificial happiness of one whose problems are so far off that there is no point in thinking about them.

De Niro's — Janice's choice — was one of those fake Italian

places found everywhere, including Italy, with misplaced Renaissance statues of dubious proportions and plastic vines draped here and there over false arbours. The food was good. Too good, for I always rationed my food, especially after a day of strenuous walking. Keeping my weight down occupied much of my energy. Janice had walked too. We began exchanging the day's sights.

"I saw the Castle. Did you go up there? Did you see the slit in the top of the arch where they could shoot straight down at anyone coming through? Vicious."

"No. I saw the cemetery where Robbie Burns is buried. The one with the statue of Greyfriars Bobby, the little terrier. Did you see that? I love cemeteries."

"No. But did you get out on the heath? It was gorgeous. The Sheep's Heid is the oldest pub in Edinburgh. And there was a little church over there that has iron handcuffs built into the wall for women who got out of line."

She bent over and inspected my black slingbacks under the table. "You walked all day in *those*? You must be masochistic!" Her shoes were sensible.

"Yes," I said defensively. "They're the most comfortable shoes I own. They're just fine for walking." She rolled her eyes as she leaned back in her chair again, signalling either amusement or disapproval. I couldn't tell which.

We couldn't talk fast enough, each one interrupting the other to compete with more shared experience, more colourful anecdotes.

"Are you married?" I asked.

"Yep, for almost twenty years. David's ten years older than me. He's fifty-four. I expect to be a widow someday. Maybe soon. All his family die young. Bad hearts. Look forward to it, actually. I plan to spend my last days alone in a little house in the Scottish Highlands. People are generally a disappointment. Better not to expect anything from anyone. He was my prof in grad school, actually. That's how we met. He's a cute little short guy with great buns. We could hardly keep our hands off each other, but we did until the end of term."

"Oh yeah, I was married to a prof of mine, too. I was crazy about him. It didn't work out. I was in first year and he got me pregnant. In those days it was just shameful ... and incredibly painful. I gave the baby up. It was terrible, but at least I can talk about it now."

She looked at me carefully without comment. "Are you married now?"

"Yes ... for fourteen years." I weighed carefully whether to tell her more. Everything in me said DON'T.

"Kids?"

"Yep. Two by the prof. And another by my present husband, Paul. Bea – Beatrix – she's twenty-one, and Hugo, he's nineteen. The youngest is Henry, he's only twelve."

"My guys are nine and thirteen — Anatol and Leopold."

"The Anapests," I said.

We laughed. Who else had kids with such weirdo names? Who else would see that the names of her guys were in the anapestic metre of poetry? Long, short short.

And what did our husbands do?

"Mine's in African history," I went on. "A Marxist. Economic history at York University. He took me to Niamey in Niger once, with Bea and Hugo, right after we were married. It was horrible. A city of thousands on the southern edge of the Sahara with no sewer system; hordes of beggars assaulting you physically whenever you went out; lepers lying on skateboards. I swore I'd never go back, and I haven't."

"That's amazing — I've actually *written* on leprosy, 'Leprosy of Lust.' My M.A. was in Latin American history but my Ph.D. was in medical history. And *my* husband's an economic historian too. He's in charge of DID, the Division of International Development at the University of Calgary. He goes to Bhutan sometimes, but I never go with him. We lead fairly separate lives. He lets me do whatever I want. That's why I chose him. 'Trip 'em and lay 'em.' That's my philosophy. After growing up in a family of three boys and a father who was an Anglican priest, I wasn't getting into all that patriarchal shit again. No man is going to push me around. My mother always said that I'm her only son. One of my brothers is a policeman, another is an engineer, and the youngest is a banking consultant."

"Well, I wouldn't know about that. I come from a family of all girls ... including my father." She laughed, a deep, warm belly laugh. "What I mean is, my father is a gentle soul. He was in the army until I was five. Even later, when he was there, my mother brought us up. Maybe it would have been different if one of us had been a boy. Then there was Aunt Winnie, his sister. I adored her. She never married, and I was her favourite. What exactly do you teach?"

"I teach Canadian Studies and law. I practised law for a couple of years. Hated it. It was a fucking man's world. I realized that if I wanted to become a judge I'd have to golf, and I hate golfing. Those guys will never get a life."

I looked at her more closely. She was tough, but in a tongue-in-cheek way. Funny. She was vivid. Her dark hair was cropped in one of the crew-cuts women had begun to favour. This sleek cut, like the glossy pelt of a seal, showed to full advantage a gracefully curved hairline and a sharp widow's peak. Her clothes seemed nondescript at first glance, but I could see that the eclectic colour scheme of olive green and burgundy — plaid shirt, pants, jacket — was carefully chosen and elegant in a tailored, understated way. She leaned back as she spoke. She wore almost no make-up, but the brown eyes that looked across at me from behind absolutely round horn-rimmed glasses were as penetrating and intelligent as any I'd ever seen.

Our small Italian waiter approached immediately after our salads were served. He hoisted up a pepper grinder more than half his own height. "Pepper for your salads, ladies?"

We both nodded, caught each other's eyes and burst into laughter. I was embarrassed. She wasn't. "Now there's a phallic symbol to be reckoned with," she said in a slow, droll voice as he walked away.

We were like two girls playing in an attic where we each had a trunk of precious mementoes. "Look at this!" one of us would say. "Yeah, well look at *this*!" returned the other. We held up one thing after another: lace dresses, feathered hats, old dolls, bits of china, broken toys, tales of our children, the delights of sex with our men, our own woes adapting our careers to theirs, the persistence involved in getting tenure — finally, for both of us, in 1990. Then the shared joys and trials of research, the details — varied and gruesome — of each birth, the exact source and meaning of each name of each child, her theories about patriarchal society, my theories about dieting, our favourite music, colours, novels, movies.

When we finally looked up, our waiter was standing at a discreet distance holding the bill. Elsewhere, the lights were out. We were the only ones left in the restaurant.

THAT NIGHT I WAKE abruptly before dawn in the sweaty grip of a hot flash. I'm trying not to cry as I float into consciousness and fumble to retrieve the dream that gripped me. It was about Paul. It is his forty-eighth birthday today, I remember. The day when he catches up to my age. He doesn't like to think of me as older, even four months older. I must call him today.

In this dream, a nightmare, Paul is storming upstairs, a stream of invective trailing him like a sulphurous cloud. "You fuckhead," he shouts over one hunched shoulder. "You turd." I feel guilty. Shamed. I have made him mad again. A door slams. A glass clinks. I am filled with cold dread, as if something liquid is being poured into the open top of my head. A door opens. Out he stamps with that look on his face. A black scowl. His loose lips shaped into the down-turned grimace of a kamikaze warrior. I am immobilized on the stairs. He pushes me backwards, shouting at me, "Look what you made me do, you stupid shit." He follows me down to where I lie in a crumpled heap, trying to make myself shrink into the smallest space. He straddles me, bends over, thrusts his face right into mine. "See? You're ruining this marriage. Get it, bitch?" I say nothing. He hits me. Hard. Across my cold cheek. Then he storms up the stairs again, and it's over.

Through the chintz and lace heavy over my window, light begins to dawn. Another sunny day. I will walk until it rains. I have to meet one of Paul's colleagues, an Africanist from London, at Bell's for drinks to deliver some research papers and a number of messages from Paul. And Janice and I have agreed to have dinner again at De Niro's.

THE SECOND NIGHT at De Niro's was even more engaging than the first. Our paths had crossed on the Royal Mile that morning

— she heading for the Castle, which I'd already seen, and me heading for Holyrood, which she'd already seen. My first impulse was to ask her to join me, but I needed time to think. Besides, I thought selfishly, I want to choose where I go, sit quietly in the sun if I can, move at my own pace. I had to steel myself to call Paul later. So we laughed at the coincidence of meeting, then went our separate ways.

But encountering her in the sober light of day sharpened my anticipation of the evening to come. I couldn't wait to compare our impressions of the two castles, and I figured her views and ideas would cast my own afresh. What would make her swear this time, I wondered. Facing each other momentarily on the Royal Mile — she dressed sensibly in mannish trenchcoat and pants, me looking like a misplaced model in my light wool suit, black stockings and slingbacks — we seemed to strike a balance somehow, like the little figures on old barometers that go in and out by turns.

Everything she said about the castles at dinner fascinated me. Her animated conversation, punctuated by salty expressions like "I'm an independent kind of guy" and "Fuck 'em if they can't take a joke" (a quote, she informed me, from Bette Midler, whom she resembled in some odd way), drowned the sound of Paul's choked, anxious voice on the phone responding to my forced birthday wishes with a plea to come back early. Everything she said about *anything* fascinated me. She had a way of turning convention on its head. Her command of feminist ideas was breathtaking. But just when I thought I'd grasped her point of view, she'd take a 180-degree turn to express a well-thought-out criticism of the women's movement.

How could I ever catch up? I had spent the last twenty years blinkered in archives or focused on interviews about my three literary lions: Hugh MacLennan, Irving Layton and now Earle Birney. The rest of the time had been for children, husbands and students — more or less in that order. I had never had enough time for any of them. Certainly no time for the subtleties of the feminist movement which — I was vaguely aware — had been gathering momentum somewhere in the background of my life. My private life, I began to see, was retrograde. I'd been stuck in time. A fifties housewife, sheltered from change. But my career had reeled fast forward into unforeseen success. Books. Magazine profiles. Awards. In public, I'd been too busy *living* feminism to examine it.

Now here was Janice — just four years younger — who had examined it with the incisive mind of a legal expert. That and much else. What *hadn't* she examined? I began to wonder. She'd been a lawyer for two years, and she was a legal commentator on social issues for CBC Radio. She had published articles on STDs, leprosy, influenza, pornography, prostitution, Calgary's architecture. She was busy now editing the letters of Mary Percy Jackson, the first doctor in Alberta's Peace River district. She had a major grant for her biography of Aimee, the evangelist (which, she said with glee, was driving her Anglican father crazy). She was on a zillion committees (and, as she said, she always ended up chairing them). And she was raising two kids. Any man with such a life (had there been one) would have been pompous, insufferable. But she was droll, laid-back, funny as hell. It was like meeting Gloria Steinem, Wilder Penfield, Bertha Wilson, Elmer Gantry and Carol Burnett rolled into one. I felt as if I was somewhere in the vicinity of an avalanche, not just of words but of sheer presence. I glimpsed sightlines in every direction. I wanted to follow them all at once. For the first time in years, perhaps ever, I did not need to hold back.

Ever since I could remember I had had to amputate bits of

myself so that I could fit in. Among other mothers with little kids in the park long ago, I had masked my professorship as "teaching." At the university among my (mostly male) colleagues, I was Dr. Cameron; I refrained from mentioning my children. At parties with my husband's colleagues, I joined the wives who had jobs, not careers, and spoke of recipes and family. To them I was Mrs. Lovejoy, or — worse — "Mrs. L." Even when I was on national committees judging books their men had written, I was silent. I made sure I was nothing more than a wife. I sported two credit cards: one under Cameron for professional occasions, one under Lovejoy (a name salesgirls invariably commented on as "nice" or "pretty") for my personal life. I felt most myself with unmarried career women, but with them questions of professional and domestic tensions could never be raised.

"See," I would say to Paul in frustration after compiling ridiculously detailed lists of the women we knew. "See! There isn't *one* like me. Not one." But since he never acknowledged to me that I was his professional equal, nor that we depended for many of the good things in our lives on the money I earned from my university salary and my extensive freelance writing, he could not discuss my loneliness, my sacrifices. Although I knew they existed, I had never connected with a woman like me — one who had an academic career that spilled over into the popular media, one with myriad interests, one who was also a wife and mother.

I think Janice and I had been talking of our love of opera when the whiny strains of Lesley Gore singing "It's My Party and I'll Cry If I Want To" filtered through the hum of voices and clink of dishes around us. Simultaneously we joined in. We both knew every word of the silly, infantile lyrics.

A third night — her last — seemed inevitable. A joke almost.

We'd return to the same restaurant, order the same food and red wine (which we both preferred, no matter what the food), and we'd talk and talk, oblivious to everyone else until we were the last to leave.

I have always hated saying goodbye. I stood on the cool dark sidewalk outside De Niro's mumbling something about getting together soon, but since we lived two thousand miles apart, I knew I sounded false. I was about to extend my hand awkwardly in a too-formal gesture when she said, "I need to hug you." She stepped forward, clasped me hard, then released me to make my way alone to Thrum's.

The next night — my last — I returned to De Niro's as if magnetized. I sat at the table I thought of as "ours." Instead of muzak or the likes of Lesley Gore, there was live music, a trio of music students: violin, viola and cello. Despite the usual scotches at Bell's, some cheerful chit-chat with the bartenders, Doreen and Titch, and yet another dazzling spring day in Edinburgh, I felt hollow and sad.

I had spent most of the morning in the Botanical Gardens. It was almost empty. No one in Edinburgh would have thought to go there so early in the spring. On a wooden bench tucked far away out of the chilly breeze behind large flowering bushes, I took off my jacket and blouse, reasoning that my plain bra was no different from a bikini top, and felt sensation flood back into my body with the sun's embrace. That afternoon, dopey and flushed, I walked all the way down to Leith, as if by moving I could keep dread at bay.

I thought it was the violin. Saddening me, I mean. I couldn't *not* think of my daughter Bea, now far away studying violin in the States. Estranged, she was. A stranger to me. And through her I couldn't *not* think of that other daughter, the one I gave away to perfect strangers. She would be twenty-nine now. Two amputations. First a translucent blond infant in a pink blanket handed to others — a gift I was still paying for, as if trapped in some metaphysical instalment plan; then her replacement, alienated, afar.

The waiters made a fuss of me, unused, I imagined, to seeing women dine solo. "Where is your friend?" they wanted to know. On learning she had gone back to Canada, that I too was Canadian, they kept me intermittent company throughout my meal, speaking of relations in Toronto, referring always to "your friend."

It was not until I left De Niro's that last time that terror really gripped me. All my radiant Edinburgh days were used up. Tomorrow, after giving my paper on "The Influence of the Scottish Long Poem on Earle Birney's *David*," I would cross the Atlantic and descend into the maelstrom.

THREE

OUR LETTERS CROSSED in the mail.

"I apologize once for my handwriting, and this is it," she wrote. I could hardly decipher it. She spoke of reading my two biographies. "I liked Hugh very much but found myself *loving* Irving," she wrote. "What a brave little girl you are to do live people!" She had looked up the Birney poem about Aimee.

I reiterated my invitation for the whole McGinnis family to visit in July. I was eager to show off the renovations in our house on Oriole Gardens, have someone use the guest room with sky-lights (my study) that overlooked the garden. And I wanted her to see "Fassiefern," our place on the Niagara Escarpment near Collingwood, so called after the Camerons' Scottish farm north of Fort William, where Bonnie Prince Charlie was reputed to have stayed on his way to the Battle of Culloden in 1745. Her boys were close in age to mine. I'd arrange a camping trip for them all. Her husband and mine shared interests. They could talk. By day, we could all swim in the pond or at Wasaga Beach. At night, the four of us could go dancing at '55 Special, a retro rock spot in Barrie. I explained how I had missed her that last night at De Niro's, missed "our complicated conversations."

"I don't know too many people who switch around from intellectual analysis to emotional wallowing to psychological speculation to things biographical (our subjects are somehow more real than we are) as you do." I wrote. "A kindred spirit, in other words." I wanted to see her again.

"Jesus!" she wrote back. "Do you usually invite whole families to stay on such short acquaintance?" She was obviously delighted.

She arrived with a present for me. She waited until we were alone in the guest room to offer it to me. It looked as if it had been wrapped by a three-year-old. "I'm not much on wrapping," she said. "Seems a bloody waste of time." Inside was a soft grey knitted vest with a row of huge pink tulips around the bottom. And with it a neatly typed page headed "DISCOGRAPHY," listing music as various as William Bolcom's "Graceful Ghost," Jennifer Warnes's songs, the soundtrack of *Amadeus*, Gershwin's *Rhapsody in Blue*, Kiri Te Kanawa singing *Madame Butterfly*. The list went on and on. "It's the music I listened to while I knit you this sweater," she said in response to my puzzled look. "In order. The one I really want you to hear is Ofra Harnoy playing Bruch's 'Adagio on Celtic Themes.' It's you. You're like a Celtic queen. I listened to it over and over on the plane earphones all the way home from Edinburgh. Know it?"

I didn't. I couldn't take it all in. I put on the vest.

"I knit a hair into it for good luck," she said.

"Where?" I asked.

"I won't tell you."

"This is a labour of love," I said, amazed. "Look," I called to Paul as we came downstairs. "Look what Janice made me. Isn't it gorgeous?" He said nothing and turned away.

We already knew each other better. During the past month Janice and I had written back and forth. We'd sent each other poems, sayings, jokes. I found one in the *New Yorker* of Adam and Eve astonished as a waiter pops out from behind a tree in Eden brandishing a large pepper grinder over the apple. She sent me offprints of her articles on pornography and on women in the encyclopedia. I sent her copies of my profiles of Timothy Findley, Veronica Tennant, Anne Murray. She returned love poems by women, one about a husband undressing in his bedroom.

I listened to the "Adagio on Celtic Themes" over and over. It moved me deeply. It was like a hymn. Majestic. Poignant. Filled with yearning. It made me *feel* like a Celtic queen. I drew strength from its intense minor harmonies. A sense of myself — not as someone shameful and empty, but as a woman powerful and possibly worthy.

In one of her letters, she warned of seriousness, then proceeded to explain her history of troubled friendships with women. It had been her first pregnancy that forced her out of the world of men, where she was comfortable, and into the world of women. What if she were to have a daughter? She knew almost nothing about women, didn't trust them, couldn't figure them out. At first it was the women she met at history conferences. Shared intellectual interests and budding feminist issues drew her into their fold. But still, she wrote, she had wanted something more, a closer relationship, a female friend. She had tried. But somehow she didn't have the knack. Each time, things had ended badly, feelings hurt, confidences broken. Just before meeting me, an important friendship had ended, and she had wept in the car as she drove to Lethbridge for a meeting.

"I had come to the conclusion that I was just no good at women's stuff," she wrote. "I was listening to Jennifer Warnes singing 'I'm restless, darling, I'm restless, waiting for you to look my way. I don't think that I can wait another day,' and I began to cry. I was grieving. I figured there was no point in trying again.

"I'm guessing here," she went on, "but I want to get things clear from the start. I figure neither of us is lesbian. Certainly I'm not and never have been. If you are, or have been, I'd appreciate knowing. Probably wouldn't make any difference, but in the past I never asked enough questions, so I got things all wrong. It's just that I want to be clear here that what I want from you is friendship. I really like you. I've never hit it off with anyone like I have with you."

"Nope," I wrote back. "Apart from some fumbling around a couple of times over the Christmas holidays with a friend of mine when I was thirteen, hilarious occasions in which we tried to figure out what boys might do, I have no lesbian experience. No worry on that score. So friendship, yes. You can't imagine how wonderful it is for me to meet someone like you."

We happily swam, walked, danced and talked our way through that July week. It was everything I'd hoped for. In that fine Ontario summer, our children camped, our two husbands — mine large and loud, hers small and soft-spoken — talked of God knows what, and she and I hiked the back roads in search of apples to cook, talking and talking and talking. Every evening we gathered round the big table overlooking the gentle swoop of the Creemore valley and shared big dishes of pasta, barbecues, the season's vegetables, my baked bread and wild fruit pies.

It was a full moon the night before they left. Janice and I finished cleaning up late. The men were out on the deck having coffee and admiring the view: layers of plummy darkness sparked with fireflies beneath the moon. We began to say our goodbyes, unaware that they were watching through the glass door. We hugged each other long and hard in the white moonlight.

"This has been wonderful," she said. "Thank you."

Awkward, as always at farewells, I blurted out, "I wish I could be a masseuse so I could fix that hip that bothers you when we hike."

"I'm going to a chiropractor as soon as I get back. I want to get into shape so we can hike again together," she said, giving me another hug and pulling back to look into my face.

The next day she was gone.

FOUR

"YOU AREN'T TAKING this seriously." It was the November after the McGinnis family visit. Our counsellor looked directly at Paul.

Thank God, I thought, an onlooker for the moment in the third chair of the tense triangle known as marriage counselling. If she challenges him, he can't shout back accusations that I have PMS, that I made him angry, that it's all my fault. Maybe *now* he'll realize that he has to change. Realize what he could lose. Acknowledge what he's done.

Paul got that jaw-jutting pout on his face and spat out at her, "I don't have to take that shit from anyone." He stormed out of her office, slamming the door so hard pictures wavered on the walls.

The counselling had been my idea. I wanted this marriage,

the life we had built up over fourteen years. I was grateful he had taken on Bea and Hugo when they were small — six and four they'd been when we met. I had overlooked a lot for that. Like the court settlement of $7,000 he owed his first wife and never told me about until a lawyer called out of nowhere when I was pregnant with Henry. We were close to broke then, and it had been largely my money that paid her off. I did not complain. Somehow he convinced me that Marcia was a vindictive predator. It would be several years before I used my research skills for my own purposes. Several years before I learned from court records in Madison, Wisconsin, that Marcia had successfully sued him on grounds of "cruel and inhuman treatment," that the court had held her responsible for costs, that between 1972 and 1978 he was under a court order he ignored to pay her $200 a month.

Paul and I met in November 1976, and married five months later. I resigned my tenured job at Concordia in Montreal to move to Toronto, where he taught. My Montreal house had served as collateral for a mortgage on the Toronto house we bought in Deer Park, an upscale part of the city. I never thought to ask why Paul, at the same age and with no children, was so much worse off than I was. He had a loan on his Datsun, no savings, no property and no clothes — not even a suit — other than African dashikis and corduroy pants. He'd spent the four years between the end of his second marriage of less than a year and meeting me researching in Nigeria. Maybe, I reasoned, he just hadn't had time to settle in properly in the four months since he'd returned. Anyway, these deficiences had seemed insignificant in exchange for sexual delights and the companionship of a man my equal in age and profession who wanted to share my children. He seemed to need me. Need an instant family. He cried when I made his first birthday party — a small family dinner with a cake I'd baked and three little presents — saying he had never had such a nice birthday. He had erratic fits of temper, but I kept telling myself that love would make him secure, calm him down.

Things had gotten worse — much worse — once I finally got tenure and a salary close to what I would have had if I'd stayed at Concordia. It had taken ten long years of underpaid teaching at the University of Toronto.

Now, sitting in the counsellor's office, I began to cry. I knew what would await me at home. Knew as much as anyone could know, given that the one predictable thing about Paul was that he would be unpredictable. It would hurt, whatever it was — an unexplained absence of a couple of days, an angry tirade, heavy drinking, forced sex, a refusal to do any of the tasks that were his.

We would have to miss the next session. Paul was driving to a conference in the States. He would be giving a paper, as usual, on slavery in Africa — precolonial West Africa to be exact. Slavery is his specialty.

It was mere coincidence that Janice was to arrive while he was gone. She was in transit from Winnipeg, where she was giving the keynote address to the University of Manitoba's law school on prairie women in legal history, to Ottawa, where she had a meeting of the National Council on Bioethics in Human Research (NCBHR, which she pronounced N.C. Bear) and another paper to give at Carleton's law school, this one on AIDS and STDs.

It would be a relief to have Paul gone, a pleasure to have Janice there. There was much I wanted to talk to her about — especially biography. She had ideas about life-writing I'd never thought of. And she wanted to hear my views, too. She had told me of the impression my talk in Edinburgh made on her. She remembered clearly meeting me at the registration desk before my session. She said she remembered shaking hands — mine so big, hers so small. The way I had moved into the handshake, then back, betraying vulnerability. "I'm a sucker for vulnerability," she said. Someone had told her I was a big deal, famous. This had sent her into flight. She wanted nothing to do with me — not going to kowtow to the central-Canadian star from Toronto. Then, she said, she listened to me speak and knew she had misjudged me. She saw I was real. That when I laughed it was true. That I didn't try anything fancy, that I let my vulnerability as a woman and as a biographer show. Standing there in my tailored suit I had reminded her of those old forties movie women. Her own first models. Garbo. Bergman. Dietrich. Hepburn. When someone asked me how I could presume to understand a male subject, I had said, "I've been hurt by women too. I know how that feels." "Now that was something I could identify with," she said. She had made a point of seeking me out at the reception afterwards.

She had one or two other friends to see in Toronto and I had papers to mark. But still, we agreed gleefully, there would be time in between her arrival from Winnipeg on Friday and her departure for Ottawa on Monday to take some walks and go out as we had in Edinburgh, even if the November weather was horrid. We had figured it all out on e-mail — our new means of keeping in touch. We exchanged notes almost daily.

I spotted her at once through the glass doors as passengers flooded into the baggage area at Pearson Airport. She was wearing a splendid long red coat, military in cut, a perfect complement to her dark spiked hair. She saw me, waved, turned around to pluck her bag from the carousel. She walked slowly towards me, smiling. For the first time I noticed that she walked on sea-legs, almost limped. "It's my rheumatism, my hip is worse," she explained. "I was bedridden for several months as a child, feverish and drugged." I imagined her as a child: dark, serious, alone in bed. Curiously I felt maternal. Wanted to heal her pain. We hugged each other, laughing.

That evening we went to an Italian restaurant — a Canadian version of De Niro's — and resumed the high-octane conversations we'd had there, as if this were another dinner in sequence. Now we had met each other's families, all but Bea. Now we had read each other's work. Now we had exchanged a few letters and odds and ends we knew the other would like. Now we had what seemed like a large store of shared experience — some of it beginning to unfold on e-mail — that drew us close and fuelled more questions and observations.

We were in the midst of a stream-of-consciousness conversation that involved Anatol and Bea's violins, our husbands' foibles, anecdotes about teaching (I was telling her about the guy who burst into my office clutching a brown paper bag and said, "In this bag is everything I believe in," and opened the bag to reveal a crucifix wrapped in chains), when she said: "I've always wanted to hike the Pennines. Would you like to make a trip of it sometime?"

Without hesitating a moment, without my usual "I'll have to check with Paul," without even knowing where the Pennines *were* (I guessed Italy), I said, "Yes ... yes. That would be great. I'd love to."

For the first time, I didn't care or fear what Paul might say or do. I had always been careful not to flirt or give any reason for complaint, but what objection could he possibly have to my hiking with a woman friend? Now that two of the kids were away at university, and Henry was a teenager, I had the luxury of free time. He knew I'd leave the fridge stocked, the clothes laundered and ironed, the house in good order. We had a cleaning woman. I couldn't imagine *anything* I'd rather do than hike all day with Janice and settle in to a good meal in the evening, just like Edinburgh. I didn't care *where* the Pennines were, I'd go.

"Where *are* the Pennines?" I asked.

"England," she said, with a look of disdain. "Right up the middle like a spine. Haven't you seen pictures? It's spectacular. I like the bleak bits best. God, I love *bleak*! The northern part along Hadrian's Wall. I've got guide books, I'll send them so you can see. God! Someone who *wants* to get out and *do* something! I got my guys to go for a family trip to Ireland, and they just sat in the car while I tramped around looking at ruins and the most gorgeous scenery."

Neither of us wanted the evening to end. I suggested Studebaker's, a fifties dance place Paul and I sometimes went to. Janice declined. Too noisy. She wanted to go somewhere where we could keep talking. And she wanted to walk, even though the Toronto streets were dank and slushy.

I decided to take her to Scaramouche because it was Glenn Gould's favourite restaurant. And the talk went on: Glenn Gould ("Did you know his fave singers were Petula Clark and Barbra Streisand?"), Toronto restaurants ("*so* pretentious!"), walking city streets ("It's great entertainment, and the price is right") until we were there. We took up two stools at the bar and ordered two scotches that together cost close to the price of a full bottle. Behind us the pasta bar, as always, was full. Full of trendy Torontonians in understated designer clothes. Behind them the south window framed the iridescent lights of the city, and beyond that, the flat black lake.

"We make a handsome couple," Janice said. I had no idea

what she meant. It couldn't be a come-on. She had spoken boldly of sex-play with David, more boldly than I would have dared. I decided she was just onto one of her outrageous observations. I laughed. I felt a warm rush. The scotch, I supposed. It was such a novel thought. Two women as a couple. I studied us in the mirror over the bar. We *did* make a handsome couple: her sleek dark hair and red coat next to my blond head and black cape.

She became more serious. The subject had definitely turned to sex. "Sex?" she said, as if she were referring to shovelling snow or knitting. "Shit, I was introduced to sex *real* young, like when I was three." I sensed bitterness, but she seemed to be exaggerating to make a point. The point being that I — whose husband pressed me for sex at least daily — was naive and she — whose husband waited for her to give him the word — had been worldly wise as long as she could remember. Paul's sex-play had become something I did not want to share — even with him. It hadn't started out that way. My mind barely brushed the thought, like a sleeve catching a burr.

"My God!" I replied. "I didn't even understand many four-letter words until I was in my twenties. And I was *married*, for God's sake. I remember kids yelling what I now realize must have been 'Bastard!' I always thought they were saying 'Alabaster!' a word I'd come across in my wide-ranging childhood reading." She laughed, I giggled. "I could never figure out what was so horrible about being called a piece of white marble."

She stopped laughing. "No, seriously," she said. "I've never told anyone else."

As we walked home from Scaramouche, she took my arm. Even though it was late, I was afraid my neighbours might see us, might report something — anything — to Paul.

"I think European women are great," she said after a while.

"They walk around like this all the time. Arm in arm. No one thinks anything of it. Nor should they. Our society is set up to keep women from connecting. We're all trained to think catching a man is a big deal. Says who? It's *men* who want to get married. Women are the ones who sue for divorce. In 80 percent of cases these days, I think. As long as we buy into this, women will view other women only as competitors for the big prize. Divide and rule. That's what the patriarchy has managed to accomplish. Behind this, of course, is a tremendous fear of the power of women."

It was heady talk. Ideas that had never crossed my mind. A view of myself trapped in a system I'd never considered, like being stuck on a crowded, littered hiking trail while clear trails nearby opened onto pristine scenery. It was late at night. We were full of wine and scotch. I almost confided that I was considering divorce. But I was afraid. Afraid to spoil some kind of balance. Afraid she'd drop me. Her marriage was obviously wonderful. Some people think divorce is contagious. They don't want to catch the virus.

When we got home, she followed me upstairs, still chatting. Instead of going down the hall to the guest room, she came into my bedroom.

"Well, good night," I said. "Nice evening. Wonderful, actually."

She looked right at me. "Good night," she said. "I love you," she added quietly. We hugged, then she turned and left the room, closing the door behind her.

I felt light-headed. Love? She had said, "I love you." Or had I imagined it? She had spoken so quietly, left so quickly. She's something else, I thought. The things she comes out with! Still, friends *do* love each other. And it felt good, very good, to be told so.

THE NEXT MORNING she was off early, seeing friends, checking out Toronto's downtown, having goulash soup at her favourite Toronto restaurant, the Korona on Bloor. It was a run-down old place with fifties booths and a clientele of European immigrants and street people. Like me, she preferred good food in a place like that to trendy places like Scaramouche that catered to what she called "victims of gastroporn." I wished she had asked me to join her. But she wanted the walk, and she wanted to be alone.

That afternoon we screened the video biography of Marlene Dietrich. Janice had suggested *Marlene* when I asked her about movies for my biography class. I had wanted to include a film biography along with Boswell's Samuel Johnson, Goldman's John Lennon and Stevenson's Sylvia Plath. But I knew almost nothing about film, something Janice knew so well that endless film trivia peppered her conversations. Her views were unorthodox, to say the least. Her favourite movie was *Roughly Speaking* with Rosalind Russell and Jack Carson. "He was from Newfoundland," she informed me. "Did you know that Marjorie Main — you know, Ma Kettle — was lesbian?" Or, she would say, "*Casablanca* is really not about two men deciding which one of them gets Ingrid Bergman. The real romantic ending is Bogart walking across the tarmac with Claude Rains."

Janice had seen *Marlene* long ago. And she had seen most of the movies Dietrich had made. "I was *raised* by movies," she claimed. "I used to get up and watch old movies in the middle of the night when my family was asleep. Garbo, Dietrich, Bergman, I knew them all. That's how I wanted to dress — not in all that frilly nylon stuff my mother wanted me to wear. I agreed to let my hair grow long for the grad prom, but the next day I went to a barber and got it cut in a duck's ass like the guys.

"You'll love this," she insisted as *Marlene* began, while Henry did his homework on the dining-room table nearby. "It would be really interesting to teach because Dietrich refused to co-operate with Maximilian Schell, the director. He was in *Judgment at Nuremberg* with her. I think he was her lover. Besides … Marlene Dietrich is a great dame. You should see her in *Blue Angel, Destry Rides Again* and *Witness for the Prosecution*. I want the song from *Destry* sung at my funeral. The one where she strides up and down on the bar in a cowgirl outfit." She proceeded to belt it out in her deep voice: "Oh, see what the boys in the back room will have, and tell them I died of the same."

The two of us settled in on the small couch in front of the TV — she wrapped in a blanket, me armed with paper and pencil to jot down notes for teaching. She didn't mind if I rewound the tape to get quotes word-perfect.

I recognized Dietrich, but that was it. I had never heard her sing or seen any of her films. I was galvanized. She was glamorous and mysterious. Her low voice was the essence of seduction. The clips from her films gripped me: the rollicking bar girl of *Blue Angel*, the devilish cowgirl in *Destry Rides Again*, the alluring seductress in *Morocco*. Maximilian Schell had devised an ingenious mosaic of images, sound bytes and time frames to cover for the fact that Marlene refused to be interviewed on film or to co-operate in other ways. It was a heady combination of Dietrich's presence, skilful juxtapositions and the most vivid example of the tug-of-war between biographer and subject I'd ever seen. I concentrated hard, stopping the tape from time to time to write down dialogue. The air felt electric.

Gradually I became aware that I wanted to touch Janice. To put my arm around her shoulder, perhaps, or lean against her or take her hand. Gestures that would have been natural with Bea when she was little, or with Hugo and Henry for that matter. But

Henry's presence behind us felt censorious. And even had we been alone, I would not have risked making an idiot of myself. Such gestures might have seemed more than they were: indications of simple affection, a need for the physical connection that had gradually been severed as my children grew away from me. As Paul got worse.

Well into the film came a scene from *Morocco*. Dietrich was singing in a nightclub dressed in tails, as I remembered her from photos. Under the top hat, her blond curls were fetchingly girlish.

"Hey, I wore tails to my law firm's annual party," Janice commented wryly. "The invitation said 'Black Tie,' so I took them at their word. David thought it was wonderful. He insisted on taking pictures."

Dietrich finished her song with an impudent flourish and saucily plucked a rose from the chignon of a sultry, dark-haired woman sitting near Gary Cooper, acting a dashing French legionnaire. Suddenly she bent over and kissed the woman full on the mouth. Then, with a cocky tip of her top hat, she swaggered back to the stage and tossed the rose to Gary Cooper — to the obvious chagrin of the woman she'd just kissed.

I stopped the tape. I found it difficult to breathe. I rewound to get the dialogue, but it was several minutes before I could speak. That kiss on the mouth made me feel strange. It was the first time I'd seen women kiss like that. I rewound the tape again. Janice laughed — at Dietrich for her saucy behaviour and at me for my fascination with it.

That evening both our husbands called: Paul from his conference in St. Louis, David from Hong Kong. We were meticulous in giving each other privacy to talk. The sound of Paul's voice made me feel queasy. He had been drinking. It reminded me of the reality I had shelved for these few days. The conference was great, he said, his words slurred. His paper had gone well. He had forgotten Janice was visiting. No reference to our counselling. A perfunctory exchange of "Love you" — "You too" and he was gone. Was he really just checking up on me? If I hadn't been home, would he have grilled me? Where had I been when he called? Who with? He'd done that before. Now he'd go back to the intoxicating sense of importance that being among other Africanists always gave him.

While Janice spoke to David, I went to my bedroom to begin listening to a tape from Esther Birney providing answers to my written questions. As usual, Esther was candid: sarcastic, angry, pained and philosophical by turns. I loved hearing her tapes. I had begun to find her story more interesting than Earle's. I was focused completely on Esther when Janice knocked on the door, then came in.

"Listen to this," I said excitedly. "I want you to listen to Esther. Her story is really unbelievable. Earle's treatment of her was incredibly cruel. I don't know how she stood it."

Janice sat down on the edge of the bed as Esther's stentorian English voice filled the room:

> So when Earle came home ... by that time he'd moved Ikuko to Dorothy's ... I said to him, "I must ask you to leave. I don't want any more of this nonsense going on," and Earle's temper flared and he said, "You and I have talked about this before and you said I could stay until the end of the year," and I said, "Yes, but I've changed my mind," and he was so furious that he took off the heavy winter boots he was wearing and threw them right across the room ... not at me, fortunately. But he packed

a couple of bags and left and went to live with Ikuko in a flat a stone's throw from my place on Comox. I'm not sure who told me, Elspeth ... either Dorothy or Earle ... that when I'd been so complacent about their going to Bowen while they were getting into Earle's car Ikuko had said to him, "Esther will win because she's taken this all so calmly ... she must be feeling very comfortable," and she had the nerve to come to me later on and complain that Earle was coming home too much! I don't know what was going on in Earle's mind, Elspeth. I don't know how much he cared for this girl. I suppose it was another conquest and he went ahead with it ...

I FLICKED OFF the switch.

"There must have been something in it for her," Janice observed. "Why do you think she hung in there when the marriage was clearly horrible?"

I felt uneasy, defensive. "Well, she liked his friends. All those poets, artists, musicians he brought home. Her family in England were too far away to help. She was worried about their son. What divorce would do to him."

"Mum ... Mum." It was Henry calling. I went to help him with his homework.

Janice was in the dim hall when I returned, waiting to say good night. She opened her arms as I opened mine. We were almost exactly the same height. In the dark hallway we hugged and did not let go. It felt so good, so safe, so comforting in her arms. She kissed the side of my neck lightly. I brushed a polite kiss across her cheek. Then she drew back at last, said good night again and walked down the hall to my study.

I went back into my bedroom and shut the door. Marlene, Esther, Janice. I felt smothered. I fell to my knees and put my head down on the bed where she had been sitting a few moments before. Warmth. I felt as if I had been struck hard by an invisible hand from above. A soft blow, as if with a feather pillow. Feathers that threatened to suffocate me. I could not get up. All I could think was, "I want to sleep with her." Nothing could have been clearer than this simple, single thought. "I want to sleep with her. I want to walk down that hall and slip into bed beside her. I want to lie in her arms. A horizontal hug. All night long."

I was absolutely shaken. What was going on? It was not sex. Sex was not part of my wish. God knows I had enough sex with Paul. I was more than satisfied physically. It was just that with Janice I would be safe. Like all those years ago when I slept with my aunt when I visited her for months at a time, her ample body and affectionate words giving me strength for the day, healing my hurts. Regression, I accused myself, quick to analyze after years of therapy. Anyway, what on earth would she do if I just showed up like that? I figured she'd treat me gently, but she would probably point out to me kindly that this was not a good idea. Or worse, she might say, "What the fuck do you think you're doing, Cameron?" Probably, I thought, she was going to bed missing David, his words from that night's call in her mind and heart. Intruding on her like that could end our wonderful friendship. Spoil it. And she would be cornered, a guest in my house. It wouldn't be fair.

Still, everything in me wanted to walk down that hall. It took all my strength to resist the urge to do it.

"Write something," I said severely to myself, echoing the advice of therapists. "You're a writer. Write it down. Fantasize on paper. Exaggerate. Get it out of your system and onto the page.

Then destroy it."

I had often had the experience of discovery through writing. Frequently I did not know what I was going to say until I composed words for the page. At times, this process seemed magical, as if it were the pencil, the typewriter, the computer doing the composing. But no revelation had ever equalled this.

"Dear Janice," I began,

I want to sleep with you. I want to walk down the hall and slip into bed beside you. I want you to hold me the same way that you hug me. I want to lie in your arms all night. I need comfort. I feel safe next to your full womanly body. When you kissed my neck tonight I felt as if I belonged with you, belonged to you. If only I could sleep with you I would be able to bear the pain in my life. You don't even know that there *is* pain in my life, but that doesn't matter. Why can't we sleep together? I wish we didn't have husbands, children. I wish we didn't live so far apart. If we didn't have families and we lived in the same place I would want to live with you. I think I would want to make love to you. I think I would want to show you with my hands, my mouth, with words and wordlessly, how I admire you and care for you. I want you. I love you....

I WOKE THE NEXT morning to reread this letter in horror. I knew I wasn't lesbian. Yet my fantasies for the first time had run wild in that direction. Fantasies, I told myself firmly. That's all it is. Anything is possible in fantasy. I destroyed the letter.

But all day I thought of Janice. She would be in Ottawa now. Today she will be giving her lecture, attending her meeting, I thought. I tried to sift what I really did want from the fantasies of my letter the night before. What *was* this all about? Nothing had ever brought me breathless to my knees before. Nothing. No one. Never.

That night I made a decision. If I phoned and asked her, it wouldn't be as bad as asking her at home. Still, it was a terrible risk. I had no idea how she would react. But she would not be my guest. She would not be cornered. She would have time and space to think. It would be impossible to act impulsively. We would not see each other again for months.

I did not have her hotel number or even the name of her hotel, but David would. I phoned Calgary. I got Leopold. He gave me the number. I braced myself and dialled. She answered.

"There's something I want to tell you." I plunged right in before I lost my nerve. "I want to sleep with you."

"Well, *that's* interesting," she said.

"I mean *sleep* with you," I stumbled on, "... as in share the same bed. You know what I mean?"

All I can remember is that she didn't say "No." She wasn't angry. She wasn't going to turn it into one of her outrageous stories: "Well, I was once propositioned by a woman — by Elspeth Cameron, actually — who called me out of the blue at my hotel. Hardly even knew her."

She said she'd write me a letter.

FIVE

IT WAS MY FORTY-NINTH birthday that January. Capricorn. The lecherous goat, the willful worker, the mountain-climber.

The more I thought about it, the more I began to identify with Birney's David. Was I, too, going to climb too high, lose my footing, downslide to disaster?

I saw Janice that month for the first time since my November call to Ottawa. She'd written me right away after that. She had not drawn back, but she had been wary. I had suggested a trail we might follow. She did nothing more than look at the map. But she had not said no.

I greeted her more carefully than ever before when she arrived on my doorstep in her red coat, her face pressed against the frosty glass door, white breath streaming from her mouth in the crippling cold. I didn't want to overwhelm her. And I didn't want anything to show to Paul.

She gave a class in my biography course. I sat off to one side. She leaned back in her chair, entirely comfortable with the tapes, slides and photos of Aimee's outrageous gospel performances and even more outrageous private life. Aimee, she explained, had simply disappeared once for a month. Just swam away one night and reappeared, barefoot, staggering out of the California desert weeks later. What really happened was unclear. A brief fling with a radio announcer? An escape from her managing mother? Trapped by white slavers? The facts were known, but not the truth.

I was following intently, challenged by her incisive grasp of the issues in writing a life, impressed by her idiosyncratic methods, a little envious of her engagement with the glamorous blond evangelist, when I noticed her mouth. How beautiful, I thought, with a sharp intake of breath. How utterly lovely. I lost track of what she was saying and watched instead those full, even lips which barely closed over strong white teeth. There was something compelling about the way she spoke. The way she carefully pronounced the "t" at the ends of words — even when a "t" began the next one. There was something endearing about the way she hesitated as she collected the next thought, filling the silence with "Ah ... ah ..." before going on.

Aimee disappeared. Right out of her life. Just like that. She had been poised on the brink of something. I understood. I felt the same.

What was it? I could hardly even think of ending my marriage. I wanted that marriage like hell. I was determined to show that I could succeed at marriage. I had failed twice, but this time was going to be it. The counselling was going well. I had felt safe enough there to ask Paul for changes. I wanted to drive the car sometimes, not always be the "wife" or the "navigator." I'd wanted it especially on the trip we took before Christmas with Henry to Vancouver, a city I knew from my undergrad years, a city Paul had never visited. It was mainly my trip, anyway, to interview Esther and some of Birney's friends and students.

I'd wanted a different kind of Christmas, free from convention. A week at Paul's brother's place at Old Orchard Beach in Maine, instead of the Dickensian celebration at my parents'. I'd wanted lobster instead of turkey, long walks along shell-strewn, off-season beaches where salty ice crystals glinted at the shore's raw edge, instead of Christmas carols played by Mother on her baby grand.

Paul had agreed. In return — though he didn't say so directly — he expected more and kinkier sex, blonder hair and the clothes he liked: tight jeans and sweaters, low necklines, high heels, short skirts, flashy earrings.

Now, for my birthday, he wanted to arm himself with his leather mickey of scotch and go to Studebaker's to drink and dance. He told me what to wear. I was embarrassed to have Janice see me in my brown leather miniskirt over black tights and spike heels, my freshly bleached hair loose down my back. I felt cheap, unworthy, silly. *Mutton dressed as lamb.*

The next day I made an unprecedented decision. Heart pounding in my chest, I told Paul that I wanted to show Janice Shanty Bay, the place where I'd spent summers with Aunt Winnie in her log cabin by the lake. I feared a scene. I thought he'd insist on coming along. But I was banking on the smoky, drunken sex he had taken with gusto after Studebaker's and the look of triumph he'd thrown Janice as we went out. He said he'd work.

I felt relief sweep through me like a cool breeze freshening a stagnant room.

"HERE'S SHANTY BAY," I said, driving down the lakeshore road I'd walked barefoot hundreds of times as a child. The tiny community looked strange in midwinter, snowbound, still, almost paralyzed. I stopped at the little church to see my friend David's grave. He had died of pneumonia the same summer I fell in love for the first time, with his older brother Tim. David had been twelve, two years older than me. One day he'd been there, playing Kick the Can and skinny-dipping in the chill grey mornings. The next he was gone. Forever.

I showed Janice his simple gravestone. It was the first I knew that tragedy could happen, I told her. The first I realized that life is irreversible. That it just ends.

We walked on in silence. A solitary car crunched past us on the snowy road. "Oh God," I said. "It's Tim."

Instinctively I turned away. The car stopped. Tim rolled down the window. He was grey now, his hair thin on top like his father's. His father, now skeletal with age, sat quietly beside him. "Come over and see Mum," he said. "She'd like that."

Introducing Janice, I felt as if I were returning to some more innocent time. Those long, happy summers of sheer animal health. And with Tim, those times of keen sensation. Often we had hidden together through those complicated, rowdy games of Kick the Can. Time after time we had simply sat there in our cool cave of bushes, our shoulders lightly brushing. Then one time he took my hand and I knew a delicious alertness that seemed to last forever. Later — much later — we stood on the hill after a game of Pirates in the peeling green rowboat. "You look gorgeous," he said. Nothing more.

A year or so later, after an intoxicating game of Murder in the Dark at his family's annual New Year's party, he had reached for me in the icy night on the way to the car and kissed me quickly and awkwardly, his tongue insistent in my surprised mouth.

That was all.

But here on the wall of Aunt Winnie's garage, a weathered, cryptic message: "Pidge loves Tim." My old family name. And I had.

Something went wrong after that. In the heady hothouse 1950s mix of peroxide blondes, rock and roll, long, finned convertibles and "American Bandstand," I lost love.

Love moved indoors then. Love happened in the overheated back seats of movie theatres and cars, not in the cool spray of sweet spirea. It was the crude boom of echo chambers that raised goosebumps, not the lake water so clear you could see each pebble's delicate colour and shape. Visceral thrills came from dancing so close you could feel the hardening flesh of boys you scarcely knew, or driving so fast your hair whipped back into your face, not from the strange, familiar mystery of finding again the big white rock lodged deep in the sand beneath your drifting boat.

I lost love then. And I lost myself. I was easy prey for Peter, one of my professors in first-year university. The day he saw me at registration, he went home and told his wife that Brigitte Bardot had come to Victoria College. (She had three children under four, one only a few months old, though I didn't know until later. He never mentioned them to me.) I was pleased when he told me of his comment. I had succeeded in transforming myself from "The Telephone Pole" into a desirable woman, at least in the eyes of an Oxford Brit with a Ph.D. from Yale who looked like Rex Harrison. It would be years before I realized that he was as fake as I was: the son of a Smithfield butcher who had lied about his age to get into the Navy during the war, and whose accent was bought with private school fees.

I was too dazzled with my success in self-creation to think about his. I was deeply flattered by the note he sent me soon after registration. "You have the fine, clear lines of a yacht," he wrote. I did not know until much later that he had seen to it that I was in the seminar he ran instead of in one of the others for honours students in English. I showed the note to my boyfriend Mark, last of the series I had gone steady with in high school. He was all curiosity. "Meet him," he said. "See what he does."

What he did in the space of three meetings was give me a little green-and-white-striped box of French perfume called Ma Griffe and get me pregnant.

I was so awestruck by Peter with his tattersall shirts, his dry sherry, his crisp Oxford accent and his office full of books ("Have you *read* all these?" I naively asked) that I said nothing. Together, Mark and I planned a solution. Abortion was never mentioned — or even thought of. Mark would marry me to save my reputation, and we would go as far from Toronto as we could. That meant to the University of British Columbia. Without so much as a pregnancy test, we married one March day at Toronto's City Hall, with two strangers as witnesses.

The baby didn't seem real at first. I still had not seen a doctor when she was born in October, during the Bay of Pigs panic. I just showed up at a hospital chosen by the cab driver.

Afterwards she was more than real. A tiny pink image of Peter. Flooded with milk and maternal longing, I knew I could not keep this child. Mark kept failing his third-year subjects, and he could not find even part-time work. We had no money, even for bus fare to the university; like other students, we hitchhiked from Kitsilano every day. Though my marks were good, I was not ambitious. But I could see nothing to be gained by leaving school. I knew what babies needed. I had been thirteen when my youngest sister was born. I had helped care for her. I knew I could not do it.

I lay there stunned in the hospital room I shared with three other wailing women: one devastated to have a boy instead of a girl, a young girl no more than fifteen who had undergone an emergency Caesarean and had no visitors, and an Italian woman whose baby (a longed-for son) was stillborn and whose numerous black-swathed visitors stood about her weeping and keening. The officious nuns (for the cab driver had taken me to a Catholic hospital) bound my aching breasts to stop the milk, bathed my torn body and pressed me to drink thick, yellow Lucozade, a glucose concentrate.

I put off the inevitable for three months, the hospital's limit for keeping newborns. Finally, taking it as a sign that a distant relation, a psychiatrist in Victoria, had offered to arrange a private adoption with friends of his who had an eighteen-month-old daughter and could have no more children, I agreed to give her up.

I went to the hospital with a lawyer clutching a handful of forms, who insisted I must name the baby. I chose Winifred, after my aunt. He brought along his secretary and a basket threaded with pink grosgrain ribbon, full of exquisite baby clothes sent by the mother-apparent. The nurse would hand her only to me. In a scene I still re-enact in my mind, like one of those hallucinatory slow-motion scenes in foreign films, I carried the blond, blond baby, now alert and smiling a little sideways, just like Peter, down the hall, past a statue of St. Francis of Assisi and out into the too-bright sunlight. I handed her over forever to the disapproving secretary in the front seat and got into the back for a silent ride back to my shabby apartment.

The hole in my heart would not go away. Four years later, I

went back to Peter, as intent on marriage and a child as he was on keeping me as a bohemian mistress.

In winning, I lost. Marriage three years later, and the birth of Bea, completed something for me but opened a hellish Pandora's box for him. That, and my Ph.D., the final thesis completed and turned in the day before Bea was born. Almost twenty years my senior, and ill-suited as a Brit to cope with the liberation of women that gathered force around us, he wanted a compliant sex kitten, a passport to eternal youth, a blond sexpot to adventure with, an adoring, uncritical student. I wanted to feel real again after the amputation of a child, indulge my profoundly maternal feelings thwarted for so long, move into adulthood, exercise my powerful mind.

Four years and a son later, we separated, the result of a three-day-long argument that was so silly it must have touched some abyss between us.

I had asked him to read Tom Stoppard's play *Jumpers*, which I had found funny partly because of a character who was a pompous and incomprehensible philosophy professor. After reading it, Peter seized on one of this character's lines.

"You know where he says that professors are at one remove from reality?" he opened, in his best lecture style, over drinks one night. It was May, and we were aboard a cruise ship to Norway. We had argued about the trip, a holiday Peter insisted on after his year on a Guggenheim fellowship in Cambridge, England. I had taken an unpaid leave from my job at Loyola College and had spent the year in an unheated, rat-infested, thatched cottage washing two sets of diapers, shopping for food daily, doing my best to keep a coal stove going. Hugo, who was now one, had almost died of bronchitis at five months in an oxygen tent in a London hospital. His hands were sore with chilblains. I was reluctant to leave him, or Bea. But Peter, who had spent most of his days in Cambridge lunching with scholars whose names I had only seen on literary books, or taking the train in to the British Museum to do research, said he needed a holiday. We would take the white Mercedes he'd bought at the factory in Germany to avoid duty and drive the Norwegian coast.

"You know where he says professors are at one remove from reality?" I wasn't paying enough attention. "That means," he went on, "that you are at *two* removes from reality." He waited for a receptive nod of agreement such as students give when a professor states the obvious.

I couldn't see what he was getting at. I thought the philosophy professor was lamenting his detachment. Philosophers — Hume, Kant, whoever — were engaged directly with understanding the universe. But the professor, who studied and taught their theories about the universe, was at one remove from this reality.

Peter elaborated slowly. "You're at *two* removes from reality. You're the *wife* of a professor, you see."

I didn't see. I was also a professor. Had been for two years. "No," I said, taking a position I would not abandon. "If I'm at any remove from reality, it's the same as you. I'm a professor too. It would be just as true to say that *you* are at two removes from reality because you are the *husband* of a professor. Besides, that character is just an academic joke. Didn't you think he was funny?"

He did not. More than that, he held as fast to his view as I did to mine.

Three years on my own followed my inevitable separation from Peter, and then came Paul.

WALKING AWAY DOWN the winter-white road in Shanty Bay with Janice, I longed for a thaw, for the return of my summer self. I had hidden her, disguised her, transformed her. I began to see that it had not been a triumph but a travesty. How could men love me when I had so thoroughly hidden myself away from them, given them what they thought they wanted, a shimmering illusion?

I wanted to make things right. Heal. Love. On impulse, I took Janice to my parents' house in Barrie for lunch. Surprised and cautious after more than a year of my deliberate absence, they were nevertheless glad to see me. Their brick house was unchanged: the same Victorian furniture and silver, polished to a fine sheen, the same pale-green kitchen with its long counter looking directly onto the large wintry garden, the same old black Afghan, shuffling the same round — up the front stairs and down the back, then through the kitchen — looking for her sister who had died years before. My father still played solitaire, his cards grey and stained. My mother still flitted about, darting restlessly from one task to another, never sitting still.

They liked Janice, I could see. Her dark seriousness was like my father's, as if it were she who was his daughter — the same way of sitting upright, the same short, commonsense statements, the same slow-motion gestures. Paul was not mentioned. It was like old times. Before boyfriends, before husbands. Bringing home a new girlfriend for my parents to meet. "You girls," they said. When we were gone, my father would probably make up one of his silly songs about her.

After lunch we drove across the chill afternoon snowscape to Fassiefern. We were unusually silent. She, I supposed, was absorbing what she had glimpsed of my childhood, my family. I felt the words of my call to Ottawa two months before hanging between us like the yellow-grey clouds that precede a tornado. *I want to sleep with you.*

I moved around deftly, opening up the place: sliding up the flowered navy cloth blinds, flicking on the electric heat, clanking open the black wood stove and lighting the fire I'd laid before leaving last time. The fresh smell of cedar and keen winter air excited me. Janice leaned back on one of the two couches facing each other over a battered pine chest and waited for me to offer her a drink.

I had never understood the anxieties of men before. I knew what girls suffered. Waiting to be phoned. Waiting to be invited to the Friday movie (if Wednesday night passed, there was no hope). Waiting to be asked to dance. These agonies I knew well. Now I could see that doing the phoning, the inviting, the asking was just as bad. Possibly worse. How could I formulate such sentences? What if she said no?

Besides, she was the one who seemed to be in charge. I watched her sip her scotch. She had not expected to rough it on this trip, so she was still wearing the black wool pants and motorcycle-style jacket she'd worn before my class, both too elegant for such an afternoon in such a place. *Sartorial*, I thought. She was all authority and dark emotion.

I wore my usual jeans and bulky sweater, my hair loose. It flew about like a child's as I fixed drinks, prodded the fire, rummaged for snacks. I was too animated, but I could not calm myself. I could hardly sit still on the couch opposite her. I tried to concentrate on her words, but all I could hear was her voice. For all I knew, she might have been reciting the phone book.

I became aware that it was getting dark. Soon it would be my favourite time of day, the blue hour between afternoon and evening. Soon it would be time to go. Paul would expect us for dinner. And who knew what mood he'd be in after my defiance of the unspoken rule that I must never go off without him.

I felt the bed in the next room like a magnet drawing me. If only we could lie down together. Only a few minutes. A long hug. Comfort. But I could not ask. Why hadn't she referred to my call? Why was she sitting there talking as if we were not alone, but in a public place?

Finally I said, "Has she reached the hugging stage?" I couldn't manage "you."

She got up, slowly walked around the pine chest and sat down beside me. She put her arms around me for a long hug. Then she drew back and looked into my face. Gently she leaned forward and kissed me softly and chastely on the mouth.

Why I fled from such bliss, I don't know. But all I could think of was getting back to the city, getting back in good time so Paul wouldn't get angry.

As we sped back along roads that severed snowy fields still blue under the early moon, we said nothing. Once she reached for my hand, took it, turned it over and gently kissed the palm. I could feel her warm breath, her full lips brushing, then pressing, my open hand. Images of stained-glass windows passed through my mind. Mary Magdalene washing Christ's dusty feet with her hair. Veronica wiping his sweaty brow on the *Via Dolorosa*. Lazarus rising pale from the dead. The power of healing love. *Suffer the little children to come unto me.*

SIX

IT WAS HER FORTY-FIFTH birthday that March. Pisces. The head-to-tail fish. The mystic, the imaginative dreamer, the swimmer in both directions at once.

She held off the celebration until I arrived two days later.

I was all nerves. Pulled in two directions at once. Anyone looking in would have seen a comfortable family party. David cooked pungent pasta and a cake. The boys produced amusing cards and whimsical presents. Like a spinster aunt called in for the occasion, I positioned myself on the margin.

No one would have guessed the hours it had taken me to choose a gift. No medieval knight could have considered with such care what to offer his lady. I had decided on clothes, then on a blouse, then — after surveying endless stores — fixed on a soft, cinnamon shirt patterned in pink paisley. The bold design and warm shades were just right for her dark, tawny colouring, I thought. I had done my best to estimate the size, finding a sales-girl like her and insisting she try it on to make sure.

Nor could anyone have guessed that the e-mail passing between us over the last few weeks had resulted in a plan so unconventional and contrary to family continuity that I was breathless with anxiety when I saw her waiting —— dark and sul-try in an open-necked red pantsuit over a discreet glimpse of white camisole — at the airport.

She wanted to reciprocate. That was clear. Her plans echoed mine of two months before. I would lecture to her class about biography. Afterwards she would take me to meet her parents. The next day we would drive south of the city to see Fort Macleod and the Crowsnest Pass, where she had spent her child-hood, just as we had gone to Shanty Bay. The distance was so much farther, she explained, that we'd best stay over. She'd book us into the Cedar Inn at Blairmore.

It had been sudden — a shock almost, since neither of us had mentioned my call to Ottawa for months — when she e-mailed me one evening (fortified by scotch, she later confessed): "Are we going to sleep together at the Cedar Inn?"

My answer — heart pounding — was a carefully worded yes.

As we drove through the almost shocking warmth of a chi-nook to Fort Macleod, she pointed out her favourite landmarks: the snow-dusty curves of land spiked with ochre where prairie gradually surged into foothills, the deeply etched oxbows fringed with prairie grass, the aching canopy of ever-changing sky, the mysterious layers of mountains receding like so many washes of water-colour. She loved this landscape with an astonishing depth of feeling.

And she loved Fort Macleod. "There," she said after we'd

lunched on Buffalo Burgers in the Java Shop at the bus terminal, "is the little library. I read my way through every book." It was a tiny shed in the middle of a yard. "There," she said, as we walked on through the flat, windy streets beyond which lay the endless sweep of prairie, "is the house where I lay in bed for nine months, I was so sick. That was my room upstairs. The one with the dormer window looking out over the fields. Mother used to come up and do puzzles on a tray with me." Now that I'd met her mother I could picture this. The nurse with a full curved mouth like her daughter's. Soft-spoken, but given to raucous outbursts of irreverent laughter. Determined her only daughter would be a pretty schoolteacher and marry young. "There," she said, as we pressed our noses to the glass door of a deserted bar, "see the bullet hole in the mirror? Someone was shot in a fight there. And over there," she said, pointing west, "is Head-Smashed-In Buffalo Jump. The smashed-in head, by the way," she added, in her father's authoritarian, earnest manner, "was not the buffalo — though they plunged to their deaths over the cliff — but an Indian boy who fell off a ledge halfway down, where he was trying to see them fall past. It used to be on my friend's farm. Now it's a historic site. I'd like to take you there someday. We could hike."

Then, after a drive into layers of rising hills, the softly tiered crown of Crowsnest Mountain loomed into view and we were at the Cedar Inn. I was almost sick with excitement. About what, I couldn't be sure. We carried our bags into a room like any other: two beds, a bathroom, a window over the narrow watery rush of the Crowsnest River.

Janice took off her shoes and stretched out on the bed. I immediately joined her and we turned to each other in a silent embrace that seemed never to end. She took my hand as she had in the car and kissed it — this time over and over. The palm, then each finger in turn. Never had I felt such delicious pleasure. No man had ever bothered with such delicacies. A bed? In a motel? That had meant permission for instant disrobing and sex that ended in minutes. I took her hand then. That hand as soft and tiny as a child's. Kissing it was as pleasurable as being kissed. I traced each tiny line with my lips. Probed my tongue carefully between each finger. Examined each small pink nail as if she were a newborn I held in my arms for the first time. She was perfect.

Without a word, in the golden afternoon light, she pulled down the covers and we lay together on deep yellow sheets the colour of sere prairie grass and gazed at each other. Eventually she undid the buttons at my wrists and touched the skin inside my arms. The pleasure was almost painful. I stroked her in the same way. Then more embraces. Long hugs from which I could feel her strength seeping into me. Knew that she was drawing on my vitality, too. We kissed. On the mouth. For the second time. Then again. And again. Slow gentle kisses sweet as the warm chinook winds outside. Then, comforted, we slept.

I would have stayed in that bed forever, but Janice roused me for a walk along the river before dinner. Arm in arm, and step to step, we walked to the town's end, then up to the single main street where, to my surprise, people greeted us as we passed.

I could hardly eat dinner. And afterwards, I turned my eyes from Janice undressing and putting on her pyjamas — striped, oversized men's pyjamas, it turned out — in a corner of the room. I retreated to the bathroom to change into a pair of floral pyjamas Paul liked. Somehow we got into bed without looking at each other. Then held each other tight, kissing each other's necks softly before falling to sleep.

I WOKE IN THE morning to find Janice rubbing my shoulders. Slowly she pulled up my gown and began kissing my back, gently, now in this spot, now that. It was all I could do not to turn over. My breasts burned. But I feared it would spoil this trance-like state we had entered. We had only an hour or so before we had to check out. We cherished every second of it. Touching each other as if we might break like porcelain. Looking into each other's faces as if our lives depended on memorizing every feature. Slowly kissing every part we dared: cheeks, necks, palms, inner elbows. Saying nothing.

Before leaving, convinced that Paul might somehow find out we had shared a bed, I rumpled the one we had not slept in. Who knew? He might query the staff the way they did in murder mysteries. Gather clues. See through walls with monstrous unlidded eyes.

We walked out into the harsh sunlight of reality and she drove me up to see the Frank Slide. There, suddenly before sunrise one morning long ago, the unimaginable had happened. A mountain peak had crumbled, and rock by rock, boulder by boulder, crashed down on the little mining community of Frank, floating on the cushion of air trapped under it then for miles beyond. The Indians knew. They had called the mountain "The Trembling One." But the Scottish mine owners thought they knew better. "Turtle Mountain," they named it, and they dug long passageways into its core to plunder coal.

Janice and I walked through the path etched by park officials. Reassuring signs at regular intervals outlined local flora and fauna or geological oddities with such cool detachment that the terrible, unforeseen trauma of many deaths — the undeserved deaths of those who already had endured transplantation into an alien world and suffered work that was scarcely fit for animals —

was pushed far away.

I could not read these signs. All I could see was a moonscape of horror. Those huge rocks — three, four, ten times as big as the two of us together. One alone could have crushed our breath from us. And here were thousands upon thousands of these rocks, all down the torn topless mountain, across the railway tracks, which had had to be relaid. Across the highway, which had been built over the immovable whitish-grey rubble. Right up the opposite slope, far, far into the distance. Even after almost a century, nothing could take root in those rocks.

Sometimes, I thought, things happen in a split second, an unpredictable moment, and life is changed forever.

SEVEN

PAUL WOKE UP with a start.

Groggy, I propped myself up on one elbow and looked over his grey curls to the clock. Three-thirty. "What's the matter?" I asked, sleep pulling me back down into oblivion.

"I had a horrible dream." This was extraordinary. He never remembered his dreams, so I'd long since given up telling him mine, which were detailed, bizarre, eventful. I tried hard to wake. "I dreamed you and Janice got married," he said.

I wanted to laugh. Then I realized he was in deadly earnest.

"Is that all?"

"Is that *all*? I don't want you to see her any more."

I lay silent. I had made an art of sleeping on my edge of the bed. Even though I was tall, at a hundred and twenty pounds I could take up almost no space at all. Avoid almost anything.

Including Paul, who was over six feet and nearly two hundred pounds. I shrank myself along the edge and said nothing. I was awake now. More than awake. My heart was a cage full of birds beating their wings, bent on escape. Surely the bed must be shaking in time. But he turned over and fell asleep.

The next day I e-mailed Janice, now a daily ritual. I reported on Paul's dream. "Well," she wrote back an hour or so later, full of good humour. "Let's see. Would we both wear white dresses? Tails? One of us in tails, the other in the dress? I think I favour both of us in tails. I always thought those wedding dresses were an invitation that said 'I am a pretty package. Unwrap me. I'm yours to do whatever you want with.' That's why I eloped to Paris with David. No way I was going to let my father preside, let myself be handed over from one man to another or wear one of those expensive monstrosities. With you I would want something that meant equality. Dress the same. Oh, and rings? What would you say to rings the same too? And we'd have to do the Anne of Green Gables thing. Didn't she and Diana pledge their troth or something on a bridge? I must check."

"And what about place?" I typed back, picking up on the elaborate fantasy. I got my Canadian atlas down off my office shelf. "Should we choose somewhere halfway between Calgary and Toronto? Like Winnipeg? Or what about Great Slave Lake, in memory of the kind of marriages we'd be leaving behind? At least we'd share the work if we lived together!"

"I told David about Paul's dream," she wrote in her early evening message. "We had a great laugh about it. He said he'd be glad to give me away!"

"Wow," I wrote back the next morning from my office computer, after checking my dusty old copy of *Anne of Green Gables*. "Listen to this. This is when Anne and Diana meet. They *do* pledge their troth:

> *"Oh, Diana," said Anne at last, clasping her hands and speaking almost in a whisper, "do you think — oh, do you think you can like me a little — enough to be my bosom friend?"*
>
> *"Why, I guess so," she said frankly ...*
>
> *"Will you swear to be my friend for ever and ever?" demanded Anne eagerly.... "We must join hands — so," said Anne gravely. "It ought to be over running water. We'll just imagine this path is running water. I'll repeat the oath first. I solemnly swear to be faithful to my bosom friend, Diana Barry, as long as the sun and moon shall endure. Now you say it and put my name in."*
>
> *Diana repeated the "oath" with a laugh fore and aft.*

"Do you think L.M.M. had any idea how erotic this sounds?"
"Here's what I found," she e-mailed back. She, too, had been checking out Anne and Diana.

> *"I love Diana so, Marilla. I cannot ever live without her. But I know very well when we grow up that Diana will get married and go away and leave me. And oh, what shall I do? I hate her husband — I just hate him furiously."*

She continued.

THIS is what women lose. This closeness to other

women. Girls have friendships like this, then they start dating guys. They never get close again. Our culture constructs gender in such a way that to shift from female friends to dating boys means losing your female friends. I don't know about you, but it was well understood where I came from that you automatically reneged on plans with your girlfriends if a guy asked you out. What does that MEAN? Think about it.

Friendships with women really MEAN something. Something different from relationships with men. We're hardly allowed even to HUG each other on greeting or parting. Anne and Diana show affection. They walk in — get this — Lover's Lane, they talk endlessly, they sit together, hold hands. Check this out. They're saying what Anne calls "an eternal farewell":

"Oh Diana, will you promise faithfully never to forget me, the friend of your youth, no matter what dearer friends may caress thee?"

"Indeed I will," sobbed Diana, "and I'll never have another bosom friend — I don't want to have. I couldn't love anybody as I love you."

"Oh, Diana," cried Anne, clasping her hands, "do you LOVE me?"

"Why, of course I do. Didn't you know that?"

"No." Anne drew a long breath. "I thought you LIKED me,

of course, but I never hoped you LOVED me."

You know, guys don't lose this connection with guys. They keep their buddies, they work together in businesses, on construction sites, whatever. I mean, the Old Boys Network isn't a myth. Women are only just beginning to network, to trust each other, to stop being misogynist themselves. I want to recapture that closeness. That equality. No marriage can offer it.

FROM THEN ON, we signed our e-mail — and even labelled our memos to each other — "Forever and ever." Tongue-in-cheek.

From time to time in the flood of e-mail Janice sent me, a message from Paul would show up. He was accustomed to calling me a few times a day, but the phone line was regularly tied up with the volume of e-mail, and he began to complain that my phone seemed to be busy all the time. Who was I talking to? he'd want to know. What was I doing? He had always kept close track of my comings and goings, my appointments, my meetings — much closer than I ever did of his. Now his surveillance increased.

"I am very angry about tonight," he wrote once because Hugo and I had both asked to use the phone after he had been on it for well over an hour. He'd been making long-distance calls all over the country because of rumours that SSHRC, the Social Sciences and Humanities Research Council, was to be merged with the Canada Council, meaning possible cutbacks in research grants to scholars. He was a member of SSHRC, and he did not want his committee subsumed into another one. He accused Hugo and me of "hovering" around his study, and his response was to declare that he would no longer prepare meals or otherwise participate in an "unfair home environment."

I wrote back,

> Just got your message from last night. I want to say I'm sorry for adding to what was clearly a very distressing situation for you. It must have been very frustrating not to have been able to get through to anyone last night to find out anything. I heard on the news only that SSHRC and NSERC [Natural Sciences and Engineering Research Council] have been transferred (back?) to the Can. Council. So the rumour was true.... I do sympathize.
>
> So yes, you are right. I should be more respectful of your office space. I am sorry I hovered waiting for the phone, and won't do it again. In fact, I propose a practical solution to what could be a continuing problem now that both of us are on e-mail. How about a second phone line? I plan to call and find out details today, if possible.

FOR THE FIRST TIME, Paul tried to use Janice to castigate me. "What would Janice say," he wrote, "on the eve of being appointed to SSHRC?" He had told me that he was putting her name forward to serve with him on the national SSHRC committee. It felt like a competition for Janice. They would be travelling to the same cities at the same time and staying in the same hotels and sharing the same receptions. I would be excluded. More important, she couldn't be with me alone when he was at meetings in Ottawa. It was shrewd of him — he seemed to intuit that the one bait that might lure her was a professional plum. I felt nervous, but I decided to keep out of it. She seemed pleased, and I didn't doubt her ability to make a significant contribution on any committee, no matter how daunting. I knew that to rise to Paul's bait was to ensure that he included it in his comprehensive arsenal against me, so when he had asked me for her c.v., I brought a copy home for him.

Meanwhile, the marriage counselling continued, but progress was slow.

"As our M.C. sessions have revealed," I e-mailed Paul after he told me that he was not glad to see me when I returned from giving three papers in Spain, then blew up because I told him I had moved the tablecloths to a different cupboard,

> there is a paradox. I don't believe our difficulties are caused by tablecloths. I have changed in ways you wanted — indeed demanded. You say you like this change, but it is not making you happy. You do seem to miss my dependence on you. On my part, I am experimenting to some extent with the new self-confidence and self-esteem I feel. There may indeed be times when I get too big for my boots, so to speak. I'm not used to independence either. However, because of that happiness and freedom, I feel flexible enough to negotiate compromises. To change and adapt WITH you to this stage of our lives. As you say, we need to discuss things more. I understand that when you're angry you must leave the house. But surely we must do post-mortems once you cool down.

Two intuitive thoughts. One: that this is a difficult era for couples because of feminism. That was clear to me at the Rogers' dinner party. All the couples expressed problems, yet all are long-term relationships. Everyone's having these kinds of adjustments, to very different relationships than those we saw as models. We're all having to reinvent the wheel. Two: that you have been working very hard and are stressed out, while I, too, am travelling, working hard and am stressed out.

Look ahead to how to improve things when I get back from Calgary. I love you. I think we are standing on the brink of a better relationship than we have ever had before.

IT WAS THE NEXT MONTH that threw me into crisis with Paul. We were still seeing our counsellor. The happier I became, the angrier he became. A Toronto friend had just been fired from her job, and I wanted to cheer her up. I told Paul three weeks ahead of time that I wanted to go to Fassiefern with Gail for the first weekend after my teaching ended. She and I had often hiked, with and without her husband. Sometimes Paul had come along too. I hoped a weekend of hiking would help her feel better. Paul accepted this without discussion. But as the weekend approached, he offhandedly said he wanted to spend that weekend with me "to celebrate the end of classes."

I held firm. Too often in the past, I had let him dictate my social doings. I had often cancelled out on plans I'd made after the slightest hint of disapproval from him, given in to avoid a fight. I felt strongly that Gail was not to be let down. She'd been tearful on the phone, almost despairing. It was bad enough to lose her job without having this plan evaporate too.

The weekend before, Paul pulled out all the stops. I can picture him still, sitting dejected on the love seat at Fassiefern, pleading with me to change my mind. I refused. I suggested that he make plans to have a nice weekend himself in some way. After all, I'd be only two days, one night, away. He said he had no idea what would be a nice weekend.

"Well then," I said, trying to prompt constructive ideas, "free associate. I like hiking because I spent so much time out of doors when I was a kid. I know it bores you, but I love it. What did you like doing as a kid? Maybe that will give you some ideas."

"No," he insisted, clearly expecting me to feel sorry for him — sorrier than I did for Gail — and give in. "I just feel dead inside. There's nothing I want to do. I don't want to do anything unless you're with me."

I told him to keep thinking. Something was sure to occur to him. But I intended to go ahead with my plan.

About mid-week something did occur to him. "I've booked a four-day holiday to Jamaica," he told me. I knew he'd expect me to be aghast. It was certainly extreme — and expensive. He must have thought I would throw up my plans with Gail to join him. But I had decided to support whatever he came up with on his own and refused to be baited as I had in the past. I took the line that this was exciting for him and fine with me. He needed a holiday, since he'd been working so hard. And the sun and beach would do him good. When were his flights? I wanted to know. I'd drive him to the airport if he left before Gail and I did. And I'd certainly be free to pick him up.

There was a freak April snowstorm that weekend all around Fassiefern, blown in from Georgian Bay. But Gail and I made the best of it. We spent two whole days tramping along slushy roads and climbing drifts onto trails that were ankle-deep in snow. We ate one lunch sitting in a damp school bus hut. At night we collapsed into our beds, exhausted and exhilarated. It was just what she needed.

I congratulated myself on holding firm and for not allowing myself to feel excluded or jealous of Paul's trip. I had taken him out to dinner the night before he left. I had made love to him, lovingly, twice, that night. At last, I hoped, we might be making the fundamental changes needed to make the marriage work. Even our counsellor had been impressed.

I went to fetch Paul eagerly at the airport late Tuesday night. The plane was two hours late. Paul was among the last to come through the automatic doors. I could see at once that he was drunk — drunker than I'd ever seen him. His eyes glittered menacingly. He was wearing a large white straw hat and his long grey curls had been partly braided in tiny strands and adorned with bright coloured beads. This, I knew, was trouble. Big trouble. My stomach clenched.

He didn't say much, didn't greet me fondly, didn't really look at me. I led him to the car. All the way home he slurred out the answer to my conventional query, "How was your trip?"

I learned in rapid succession that he had smoked lots of dope, gone to a nude beach, made "tons of friends," gone dancing every night, paid a woman to rub his back with suntan oil on the beach, lusted after the women in thong bikinis. He hinted that he had gone to bed with one or more women. Everyone, he said, was sexually available. He had arranged to rent a house there next April, he told me, and would invite the kids to come for a "no-rules" vacation. He meant to introduce Henry to marijuana. All in all, he told me with a bitter edge to his words, it had been "a mystic experience."

When we got home around midnight, Henry bounced up the

stairs from his bedroom to greet his father. Paul stood in the front hall and undid his bag. Everything had been stuffed in, nothing folded in the usual way; it looked like a bag full of cleaning rags. He scrambled around for presents he had brought us, but in his drunken fumblings he couldn't find them. He staggered upstairs.

When I came into the bedroom, in dread, he grabbed me and pulled me to him. Through his teeth he told me again how sexy the beach girls were. Informed me that I did not and never had satisfied him. "Now lie down," he ordered, pushing me back onto the bed. "Spread your legs." He began to tear my jeans off, but I managed to get up and say, "Look, Paul. You are completely out of control here. You sober up tonight. I'm sleeping in the guest room. We can talk tomorrow."

In the guest room I propped a chair upside down against the door so he couldn't open it. I lay down and wept.

The next day I e-mailed Janice the whole sorry tale.

"Hey," she e-mailed back cheerfully,

> looks to me like a guy who had absolutely no fun at all on his "wild" vacation. How could you stop yourself from laughing at such nonsense? Obviously without you he has no idea how to live. How pathetic! How conventional! Dope, nude beaches, thong bikinis. Sounds like the poor man's Hugh Hefner to me. Doesn't P. have *any* imagination?

I assured her I did *not* find it funny. She toned down her messages, offering sympathy, trying to get me to see it in perspective. I couldn't.

It seemed even less funny a few days later when a woman

called Bernadette with a West Indian accent phoned and asked for Paul. No, she did not want to leave a message.

I hoped that the counsellor could help us. She had taken part in all the discussions beforehand: my invitation to Gail, Paul's apparent agreement, my refusal to accommodate his request to change plans, his decision to go to Jamaica, my support of his plans, my cheerful offers to drop him off and pick him up at the airport.

I was distraught at Paul's treatment of me. So distraught that I avoided him completely until our appointment with the counsellor. Instead of tackling him directly, trying to get him to see how cruel his behaviour was, how destructive of everything he said he wanted, I spent my spare time getting everything down on paper. I went into professor mode. I analyzed as carefully as I could the implications of the situation. I made lists of what I wanted in the marriage, lists of what he said he wanted in the marriage, lists of the ways in which this Jamaica trip represented a giant step backwards for me. I described the issues as I saw them. I tried as hard as I could to put myself in his shoes — or his bare feet, as the case might be. To figure out how he saw this. I was sure that if I could get it all clear and see things from his point of view as well as my own I would understand. And after understanding, I would be able to do something to make things improve.

"Elspeth has asked me to get in touch with my own needs," I wrote down, trying to speak in his voice, imagining what he might say,

> and take some initiative in meeting those needs. Does she really mean my needs, even the ones I know are illegal (dope-smoking, adultery), the ones I've promised her I won't ever do; the ones she used to be jealous of or

get annoyed about (getting really drunk, dancing with others); ones she hasn't even considered, but which I feel pretty sure she wouldn't like (rub-downs on the beach)? What about making a decision without consulting her (renting house for next year)?

I kept posing hypothetical questions and thought processes from his point of view.

If Elspeth prefers a weekend hiking with a girlfriend to being with me, I'll just do what I prefer, whether it hurts her or not. It hurts me that Elspeth wants to do something else when she could be with me. But I don't dare complain because rationally I see that she intends me no harm. I would act too possessive. What I really want is that Elspeth stop this independent planning with others — no matter how innocent — and spend time with me. One way to accomplish this is to make her suffer for choosing not to be with me. "If you're not there with me, look what I get up to. Next time come with me."

I formulated what I thought were concise conclusions for myself.

1. P's dependence on me. How much he loves and needs me. Terror of abandonment.
2. P's vindictiveness when he feels rejected. (Breaks promise made before we married re: dope).
3. P's use of "mental cruelty" — sexual innuendo — to punish.
4. *Testing* a response to changes in me: confidence, independence, trust.

By the time we got to the counsellor's, I was better prepared than for any lecture I had ever given. I hoped he had done the same. Here, in this single situation, were almost all the difficulties I'd experienced in our marriage. It was a microcosm of my fifteen years with Paul. I believed that he wanted me, wanted the marriage as much as I did. I expected that a discussion of Jamaica in front of a therapist who had seen us interact weekly for over a year would uncover whatever dynamic between us was so terribly wrong. Then we could both make changes.

Paul slouched in his chair. I clutched my notes as if they were fetishes from which I might gain strength and confidence. Our counsellor looked from one of us to the other. Paul refused to talk, so I began.

"And what is your version of these events, Paul?" she asked after about ten minutes.

"I had a great trip," he offered. "It was the most fun I've had in years. I did everything I wanted to do, but didn't do anything that would hurt anyone else. I felt ... mystic. I found my centre."

"Were you on drugs?" she asked.

"Yep. Only dope. That's no big deal. Elspeth's always made a big deal about it. It was great."

"But drugs can induce the sense of a mystic experience."

He was silent. He had that look on his face.

"How would you describe your trip back from the airport in the car with Elspeth?"

"She hates seeing me have a good time. She hates beaches. I love them. It's about time she faced up to a few things. She's always jealous of me. I'm not even supposed to look at another woman. She just wants to control me all the time. She acts like a policeman."

"So you basically agree that you took drugs in Jamaica. And

you led Elspeth to believe that you might have been involved with women there?"

"I didn't screw anyone. I never said that."

"But how can I be sure?" I interrupted, agitated. "You broke the promise you made to me when we married — that you'd give up marijuana. It was the only condition I set. Now you say you're going to get Henry smoking dope ... want a 'no-rules' vacation back there."

"I just said I want to be there when he tries it out."

"... so I can't trust you to keep that promise, I can't trust you to be a responsible father ... why would I trust you with women? You had someone rubbing you down with oil. You had someone braid your hair. You said you went dancing every night. You hung out on nude beaches. You talked of sexy girls and how much you lusted after them. A few days after you got back there was a call for you from a woman with a West Indian accent who left only her name ... no number. You refuse to tell me who she is ... what is going on? What do you expect me to think? Jamaica is a well-known spot for AIDS. I feel as if I should get tested. I think you should too."

The counsellor turned to Paul. He said nothing.

She turned to me. "I think getting tested for AIDS is a good idea," she said, "whether or not Paul does."

Suddenly Paul turned on her. "You side with her," he said nastily, leaning forward as he so often had towards me, thrusting his face out. "You aren't objective at all. You're a lousy counsellor. She could have come with me if she cared about the marriage. She'd rather hang out with her lesbian friends. She and Gail were up there screwing their brains out. Don't you see?"

"No, I don't see. Were you having an affair with Gail?" she asked me.

"No," I said.

But I thought of Janice. Of our friendship, which had become more and more physical. Was it just comfort? Affection? Or was it something more? We had not done anything sexual, but I felt funny when I thought of "bosom friends," or when I looked at her mouth, felt odd about my pleasure in the way she smelled, and about the fantasy letter I had written and destroyed six months before. Was I fooling myself? Had I bought into Janice's theories about friendship between women, the physical ease of European women, feminism in general, when what was happening was really something else? I felt sure I could draw the line between affection and desire. And I hadn't had any sexual fantasies about her — other than that first letter. I didn't know. I was afraid, though. Not just of Paul — of myself. Afraid even to think about it. I didn't feel at all like that about Gail. I said nothing more.

The counsellor became even calmer than usual. I watched as if my life depended on it. Back and forth. Back and forth. Back and forth. His insults and her calm replies. Like some kind of psychological tennis game. And in that interchange I saw for the first time how to deal with Paul. I had always become distressed, hysterical, whiny and accommodating. She was firm, assertive, quiet and calm.

"I think you have been paying lip-service to this therapy all along," she said in a low voice.

"You bitch," he said. "Why didn't she come with me?"

"You agreed with her plan for her friend. You didn't invite her. It was all discussed right here."

"She's a fucking lesbian. All her friends are lesbian. Dirty little feminists!" he shouted.

"Elspeth has spoken of several friends, a few of whom are

lesbian, most of whom are not. I understood these were your friends, too, weren't they?"

We did know two lesbian couples, and a few male couples as well. Once we had had one of the lesbian couples to dinner and between courses, Paul had passed behind one of these women, stopped and lifted up her long, dark hair caressingly. I had been hurt. Protested later.

"Not that fucking women's group she's gone to for years. Drinking beer out of the bottle. Running down men."

"It seems to me that you are angry whenever Elspeth does anything with anyone other than you. You've said you were even jealous of her closeness to the children."

"That's not true! Liar!" he shouted. He sprang to his feet and stormed out. He would not discuss Jamaica again.

In the days that followed, Paul was almost too friendly and helpful. It was our anniversary in mid-April — our fifteenth. He wanted to get me off alone, make up, "get back on track," as he said. I wanted more family stuff. Maybe what he couldn't do for me he could do for Henry, I reasoned. Maybe if Henry were out with us for dinner, he wouldn't get drunk, wouldn't fly into one of his moods. So it was at my suggestion that we went off to a Greek restaurant with Henry.

Over drinks beforehand, Paul produced a tiny box for me. And I produced one for him. He opened his first: a pair of green onyx cufflinks set in gold. I opened mine: a gold filigree ring set with sapphires and tiny diamonds.

"I got this for you in Jamaica," he said. "I wanted something special for our fifteenth."

My stomach heaved, but I didn't let on. How could he be so thoughtful in a place where he was not only doing things to hurt me but intended to torture me with the information? How could he buy this ring at the same time as planning a "no-rules" vacation for next spring? How could he want to celebrate fifteen years with me even as he was lusting after the girls on the beach?

"I didn't do anything in Jamaica, you know that," he said in the light, ticklish, hypnotic voice he used with me when things were fine between us. "I told everyone I met there what a great wife I have. I wanted to make love to you under the moon on the beach late at night. I want to take you there, not just next spring, but as soon as we can get away. Let's do it right. And next spring, how about inviting Janice and her family to come along for a family holiday with us? I'll e-mail David and invite them tomorrow. Okay?"

I wanted terribly to believe this. He hadn't actually apologized or spoken honestly about what he had done, but his voice mesmerized me. It was like shifting to another dimension — a place where we loved each other, meant each other well, cherished a long-standing marriage. He *had* changed. I felt it in my bones. He had gone too far, been burned, learned his lesson. It would be better from now on.

The next day I e-mailed Janice all excited about a joint family holiday next spring. Told her about the ring. Explained that Paul hadn't really meant any harm, that he sometimes got like that, but this time would be the last. She was right. It really was funny more than anything else.

Her reply startled me. She was angry.

What the hell, Cameron. You get me all worried and convince me that P. is driving you nuts, then the next thing I know everything is lovey-dovey. Doesn't make sense. This is driving ME crazy. Matter of fact, I think I need a break from all this e-mail. I'm neglecting my family and I have so much work to do I can't really afford to ride this roller-coaster. So I'm checking out for a week. I hope you and P. sort your life out down there in Graysville. Don't look for me on the machine until sometime after noon the 22nd. Forever and ever. J.

I tried to convince myself that the absence of e-mail from Janice didn't matter. I had my book to write, classes to teach, and I was doing all the shopping, cooking and many other tasks at home. My days were full. And Paul — as always — made his demands at night. For the time being, he seemed satisfied. Things were calm, or relatively so. But I missed her. That e-mail was like a lifeline for me. Something certain, comforting and connected in the midst of Paul's impulses and sudden shifts of mood. But more than that, I just plain missed her. Her. Her humour, her flashes of insight, her wacky observations. Her declarations — often arcane or obscure — of affection. "Miss Cameron," she used to write, assuming personae for us both that made fun of our ladylike upbringings.

I do wish I could come to tea today. Would you wear white gloves? One of those little hats with veils? I would kiss you lightly on the cheek to greet you. Perhaps you would agree to stay over for a longer visit? Forever and ever, Miss Dickin

I continued to check my e-mail from habit, although I didn't expect to find a thing. And then about midweek there was the signal: "New mail." I might have been delighted, had I not felt so angry. I had braced myself for a week. But here she was, back early.

She herself seemed to resent changing her mind. Her message was churlish, taking me to task for confusing her and expecting her to adapt to the pendulum swings at Oriole Gardens. At the same time, she made it clear — reluctantly, I thought — that she regretted imposing a week's silence. It was too long.

I decided that I would not respond until the week was up. I was putting into effect some advice from the counsellor, intended for my marriage. "Don't allow yourself to be manipulated." "Don't respond to threats." But it was as hard for me to wait as it must have been for her.

Right at noon, Tuesday, I e-mailed her. Explained that I was not going to be jerked around by being told one thing and then being expected to fall into line at her whim. I had never stood up to Paul like this. I was terrified. I expected her to check out completely. Instead she e-mailed back her disappointment, but also her intention of going forward. She phoned that night at my request, and we had a long, difficult conversation filled with silence and pain. I knew there was much she could not possibly understand. There was so much she still didn't know.

WE DECIDED TO work together on a presentation for the Learneds that spring, the annual meetings of the academic associations. From the very beginning, I had wanted to work with her. Paul had done articles, books and presentations with various colleagues. Meeting Janice in Edinburgh had opened this same door for me. At last I had found a scholar with abilities that complemented my own. I was strong in Canadian cultural studies. She was strong in Canadian history — especially social history. I had been involved in journalism for years. She was involved with feminist theory. I worked hard to live up to the high expectations she had of my ideas and talents. In the end we worked out a paper that has since been published in various forms. We were invited — independently and together — to present our ideas to a variety of audiences, national and international. Presenting with her was electric for me. Writing with her, side by side at the computer, was the most exciting work I ever did. One would start the sentence, the other complete it. One would draft bits, the other would pick up the argument as if a relay baton were being handed smoothly from one runner to the next. We revised each other seamlessly.

At the end of June, Paul took Henry out of the last three weeks of his grade nine classes to go to Africa for a month. Our counsellor raised questions about his priorities. Was he committed to counselling, or not? To go away for a month before the issues raised by his Jamaica trip were explored was counterproductive to the aims he had stated when he began. She used the word "denial." And what about Henry? His marks were not great. Most of his teachers had indicated that he was not achieving what he was capable of. Couldn't the trip wait a little, at least until Henry finished school? Couldn't it be shorter?

Paul refused to change plans. It was educational for Henry. It was a better season to visit Africa. Fares were cheaper (though Paul's way would be paid by a grant, anyway). There were many reasons, it seemed. "You don't know a thing about Africa. You've never been interested in my work," he told me. "So don't interfere."

I didn't. Instead I invited Janice to stay for a week. We went to Fassiefern and hiked. We visited my parents. We spent happy, peaceful days in the first flush of summer at Oriole Gardens. We breakfasted in the early sunshine outside on the deck. I cooked her the foods I knew she loved: quiche, lamb stew or chicken livers with green peppers. We explored Toronto. A day at the Island, a walk along the Scarborough Bluffs, several strolls in the Mount Pleasant Cemetery to admire the two unfortunate ladies cast in granite at either end of a bench, reaching out to each other but never touching. And at night we shared a bed. Slowly kissing each other's palms. Gazing at each other's faces. Rubbing each other's feet. It was like loving my babies all over again. That delicious closeness. That affectionate bond. Those delicate, tender caresses. It was as far from the sex I had known with men as it could possibly be. It didn't even feel sexual. We were fastidiously careful never to touch each other anywhere "sexual." There was a line, I insisted, and as long as neither of us crossed it, then no one could be hurt. It felt like the purest of pure love. Like angels and feathers and floating in air.

When Paul returned from Africa, we immediately resumed counselling. I was alarmed at remarks he made to Henry about "our little secrets" which "your mother doesn't need to know." The counsellor urged Paul to return to the feelings he had had in Jamaica, before dealing with anything else. He dismissed this idea, saying, "We've dealt with that." He had come to the conclusion during his month away that I had been tested for AIDS (the result was negative) because I had been "screwing around." Nothing to do with him and Jamaica.

I was upset but determined to copy the counsellor's manner of dealing with him. I swore I would try to remain calm, no matter what he said or did. I would have my own clear view of things and quietly stick to it.

I stated that unless Paul faced his behaviour and dealt with it, I intended to leave him. The therapist had said, "Anyone can remain married. It all depends on what you decide to put up with," and I had thought long and hard about this. I had put up with too much. I had found the counsellor. I had worked hard at the sessions and between them. I had changed behaviours Paul had asked me to change. He had changed none. If anything, he was worse. Now we were at an impasse. I wanted the Jamaica thing sorted out, explained. The counsellor did too. He had disregarded her advice about his trip to Africa. If a trained professional was dissatisfied with his behaviour after more than a year, I could not — would not — feel guilty about leaving. The next session I announced, "I've seen a lawyer. I wanted to find out my rights and the laws about separating. I'm really serious, Paul. Please try."

During the session following he sat hunched over in his chair. In a tiny, wheedling voice I had never heard him use, he begged me to forget about therapy and stay with him. "We can do fine on our own," he said, his head waving slightly from side to side. "Therapy isn't doing us any good. I love you, Elspeth. Please don't leave." This was a Paul I'd never seen. He seemed like an ancient grey-haired infant. I felt my stomach turn. The therapist booked us an extra session for later the same week.

The next time, Paul was all puffed up like a male pigeon. This Paul I recognized. This was the Chair of History, the Associate Vice President (Academic), the Bully. Pursing his lips into a tight line and pressing his fingers together into a steeple, he announced that he, too, intended to see a lawyer. There was little room for discussion. I asked to have the house alone with Henry for a week, since I had hardly seen him since mid-June. Paul agreed. He would spend the week at Fassiefern. I felt relieved that he seemed to want to separate too. His agreement to make space for me and Henry gave me hope that we could negotiate. I suggested taking Henry out for dinner to give him time to pack.

When I returned with Henry, Paul was standing menacingly in the middle of the picture window at the front of the house. He had not left, and he wasn't going to. I went into the house, packed an overnight bag and went to a friend's — an older woman lawyer who had known about the difficulties of our marriage all along.

It was from there that I phoned Janice and told her for the first time how serious my troubles really were. Paul had already phoned and e-mailed her, she said at once. She hadn't understood what the hell he was talking about. His e-mail was jumbled and obscene. It had ended with an invitation to her to go to bed with him.

I took a deep breath. "I've left him," I said.

There was so much I hadn't told her, so much I never wanted to admit to myself. While one part of me could see Paul for who he really was, another part was too busy fabricating the illusion of a happy marriage to admit the truth.

"I should have told you long ago, but I hoped I could fix it, that it would get better. I thought therapy would make him change. He's been violent — on and off — since eight months after we married. The first time I was pregnant with Henry. He threw me on the floor and kicked me in the belly. There were other times, too. I began calling the police about six years ago. They've been to both our places. Five times in all. It's been so awful, Janice."

She was silent. I went on.

"When I met you in Edinburgh, everything was in crisis. I was terrified that the marriage was over. Three weeks before we met, the police laid charges of assault against him. His trial wasn't until June. I did my best, Janice. I tried to persuade the police not to lay charges. They wouldn't agree to this. They said it was the only way to stop repeat calls. I went to the crown attorney and tried to get him to drop the charges. He wouldn't. He said these guys never change. He was so cynical. I *know* Paul can change. Mostly he's very good to me. I was supposed to testify. He gave me a black eye and a concussion. I had a huge lump on the back of my head. He threw me on the floor and said, 'Are you satisfied now, Elspeth?' I got two subpoenas after I got back from Edinburgh, but I refused to testify. I even paid for half his legal fees."

I felt a surge of relief to have finally said it, and an almost overwhelming feeling of closeness to Janice, now that we'd shared this, too.

I paused. Janice said, "Now I understand. This makes sense. I'm so sorry, darling. Paul told me he wasn't coming out as we'd all planned. You'd better come out here alone with Henry."

EIGHT

At first, Henry and I moved in with the sister of a friend. "Go somewhere where Paul can't find you," advised my lawyer, who had dealt with many violent men. We stayed there until it was time to take the plane to Calgary.

Once there, I spent hours out walking the city with Janice, talking myself round and round in circles about what to do. I got books from the library about domestic violence, and what I read was chilling. Why had I known nothing about this? Why hadn't my therapist — a psychoanalyst I'd seen before our marriage counsellor — told me? He knew Paul hit me from time to time. He was the one who had first encouraged me to call the police when I fled the house one night and called him at 2:00 a.m. That night we'd been to the National Newspaper Awards ceremony, where I had unexpectedly won two major awards.

Paul was angry, and I was afraid to go into the house with him, preferring to spend the night in the car. But half an hour later, he stormed out, climbed in the car and unleashed a tirade and several punches in the face. "You stupid turd. You cunt," he'd yelled in my face. "You aren't going to win the Governor General's Award this year. You thought you would. Your Layton book is shit." He'd named one of his colleagues, already knew through the grapevine that he'd won it.

My therapist suggested I wear make-up and sunglasses to hide the black eyes.

And what about our Anglican minister and neighbour? He had taken me once to Sunnybrook Hospital, and on two occasions I had turned up on his doorstep, three houses away, to spend a safe night.

He advised me to think of the children.

I had never before heard of the "honeymoon cycle" — the way such relationships go through predictable phases. First comes a build-up of tension, then the need to control, finally a violent outburst, and then an apparent resolution in the honeymoon stage. But even during these times of bright reconciliation, dark tensions would begin to build again. *Jamaica*, I thought. *The night I won the newspaper awards.*

On one thing the books were agreed. The chances of changing such behaviour are almost nonexistent. Still, because of the honeymoon stage, hope for change is always strong. No relationship is more difficult to get out of than this one. And yet it must be ended.

But, I kept saying to Janice, when he's good to me he's wonderful. Presents, favours, good humour. Yes, she'd say. And that's the point. Read the books again.

But, I'd say to her, I've worked so hard to make this marriage work. I *can't* exit a third marriage. We've made a family for the kids. We've built up two properties. I'm to blame, too. I've had terrible PMS, said dreadful things when I was angry, been too dependent until about a year ago — until I went to Edinburgh, actually. Maybe I should just stay dependent.

"You didn't pick up his hand and hit yourself with it," she'd say. "Nothing ... *nothing* you could do or say deserves that. PMS? That's a physical, hormonal problem, isn't it? If he were sick, would you get angry at him? Or would you try to help him feel better? He had other options than to blow up at you. Jesus, Elspeth, I've seen you in action. I've never seen anyone work like you do. You do all the laundry. You supervise the kids. You do the shopping and cook all these elaborate meals. You even bake bread, for God's sake. He sat there on the couch drinking while you made dinner for us all at Fassiefern and said, 'Nyah, nyah, nyah nyah nyah, Elspeth's having fu-un!' The guy has no idea what he's got in you. None whatsoever."

When we got back, I returned Henry to Oriole Gardens to pack for a month away at camp in Quebec. I moved in with a friend, and met with my lawyer, who advised reinstituting the restraining order that had been in effect after the police laid assault charges a few months before. A day or so later, Henry called to say that Paul had gone off the deep end. I fetched him within minutes, after telling him to wait with his camp stuff at a neighbour's. He stayed with me until it was time to catch his train for camp.

While I waited out the couple of weeks Paul was given to move out of Oriole Gardens, I went to my parents'. They were kind, sympathetic, offered to lend me the money I'd need for what was sure to be an expensive divorce. And there, in the peace of their summer garden, I worked on my Birney biography and sent daily messages to Janice through the e-mail line I set up through a local college.

Once Paul had left, I moved back into Oriole Gardens, terrified. Gail and her husband stayed with me in case Paul showed up. I was nervous, but as the days passed before Henry returned from camp, I began to calm down. I could hardly wait until Janice came to visit the week before classes began in September.

Janice and I had seldom phoned, mainly because I had a thing about long distance. Our leisurely calls, ending with anguished silences, were expensive. And it had been dangerous. Paul could easily have listened in on one of the other two phones. I had had to insist after we married that he stop going through my purse. He walked into the bathroom sometimes when I'd closed the door. And I knew he read the kids' letters from Peter whenever he could find them. He had gone through Bea's diary. Janice had commented on the way his open study in the middle of our newly renovated second floor was like a watchtower. I had to pass by to get to mine. And my comings and goings from our bedroom were under surveillance too. As one of my other friends jokingly observed, "You're like the Princess in the Tower with her guard up there. How do you stand it? How can you write?"

When Janice called one night in August, I knew right away that something was wrong. It was in her voice.

"What's wrong?" I asked. I assumed it was concern for me. Or maybe something to do with her trip to Toronto soon.

"It's David," she said tersely. "He's had serious chest pains. He's in the hospital now. He's got to have open-heart surgery. Probably a quadruple bypass."

I felt torn. If David died and I was free of Paul ... no, no, I thought. That's terrible. Awful. She *loves* David. I don't want him to die. I want her to be happy. Have the family life I know she wants.

"That's terrible," I said. "Awful. How are the kids? How did it happen?"

She told me she was furious at him. "He's been having chest pains for a year and said nothing. Real sharp ones right around under his arms. He's such a fucking *Catholic*," she said. "He really believes all this shit about when your time comes. Nothing to do but submit to fate. Jesus! The kids are upset. *I'm* upset. We were just walking up to the tearoom in the mountains at Lake Louise on the weekend. He kept falling behind. Told us to go ahead. Then he stopped. He was so white, Elspeth. I think he almost died right there. Without saying a fucking *word*." Then she added, "I still plan to come down there, assuming he's recovering okay. I think they'll do the operation soon. That's what they say. He decided to sign into the hospital when we got back. Christ! He could hardly walk up the hill to our house. Had to keep stopping, and walk sideways, like a crab. They've tested him. It can't wait. My ticket is for a couple of weeks from now."

All I could feel was stunned disappointment. I knew she would not be coming.

I was right.

E-mail after e-mail documented the distressing process of David's operation. How the doctor called them all in and explained the risks. How some patients don't make it through the operation. How veins taken from his legs must be used to replace the ones next to his heart. Or how the incision itself would run "from stem to stern," as she said, trying to joke. How she needed sleeping pills to get through the ordeal. Then, how relieved she was that he made it okay. How she drove over every day for the five weeks he was in there and took him Egg McMuffins for breakfast. How the kids went too and were terrified to see their Papa helplessly hooked up to tubes and wires in the Intensive Care Unit. How Leopold couldn't eat much and Anatol couldn't stop eating. How her parents berated her for even thinking of leaving him for a week to come to see me.

I didn't see her again until the month before Christmas. She had a meeting in Ottawa, and I asked to join her. I had research on Birney to do at the archives there. She seemed pleased. She would stop at Oriole Gardens for a weekend, then fly out, and I would drive up to meet her at her hotel in Ottawa. I would share her room there for two nights. "Don't forget your bathing suit," she e-mailed. "They have a great pool."

BEFORE SHE CAME I e-mailed her some news, and wondered how she would react. The fact was that I had reconciled with Paul. He had phoned from the room he'd taken in an apartment hotel on Avenue Road, about five blocks from the house. In his new wheedling voice he'd begged me to have him back. He had allergies to the mattress, he said. The place was dingy. It was expensive. He hated it there. He seemed contrite. I felt sorry for him. He *must* have learned his lesson, I thought. Now, I felt sure, he would make some changes.

I put aside — into some other compartment of my mind — the fact that he'd never actually apologized for the times he'd hit or shoved or kicked me, never acknowledged the seriousness of the police assault charge over a year before, or my loyalty (if that's what it was) in ignoring two subpoenas to testify against him and paying half his legal fee of $5,000 when he'd asked. And he still would not discuss Jamaica. The books I'd read on violent men seemed remote, unreal. Less real, certainly, than the pity, love and hope I felt. Or the dogged will I had to make this third marriage work.

I told my lawyer to put the divorce on hold.

When Janice arrived, I felt a whole different atmosphere between us. She was so relieved about David's recovery from near death, all she could talk of was what I had come to think of as the McGinnis Family Narrative.

"He looks so much younger," she said, as if she had fallen in love with him all over again. "I swear his hair is less grey, darker, like it used to be. His colour is better than I've seen it for years. The sex is fabulous." Her tone was the same one she used when she told of how she and David fell in love, how they couldn't keep their hands off each other, of how they had had to wait until the course he was teaching her class was over, how they had discussed children — even their names — before they'd married, how they'd eloped and married in Paris just after Christmas. It was a heady romance, this narrative, augmented by the addition of each child. The Caesarean sections, those beautiful babies, their differing, eccentric personalities. Then later, the family trips: to drift by barge along canals in the south of France, to hike in Ireland, to lounge on the beach in Hawaii. All this carefully documented by photos — nicely arranged in albums and labelled by David.

Paul hardly spoke to her. He kept out of the way, working at his computer. Janice, apart from coolly polite comments, ignored him.

As I drove to Ottawa, my car loaded with notes I needed for my work on Birney, I felt grief. I had lost her, I was sure. We had retreated from stunning intimacy into a cooler friendship. We had moved towards something cataclysmic, then each of us had drawn back — me into a reconciliation with Paul, she into a new start with David. Was this it? Had we briefly shared a path through the thickets of mid life before finding an open space, a clearer perspective, and branching off again into our separate lives? If so, wasn't this a stroke of luck to be cherished? Two women, helping each other to regain balance. Holding each other in the dark night of the soul until day broke again. I should have been happy, relieved, pleased for her and for myself.

But I wasn't. I felt deeply jealous of David. It was terrible. I didn't want to feel that way, but I did. I couldn't bear to lose that delicate intimacy. See it turned back to him. The balance, I thought, had been upended as soon as she'd learned of Paul's violence. It had been then that she'd backed off. No wonder. No one would want to get too close to that stuff. Or was it because I was back with him? She agreed with the books, I knew that. She worried that he'd get even worse. She thought that I was a fool, a weak fool, to let him back in.

In Ottawa she was gone all day at her meetings. I did what was needed at the archives, then wrote away on my biography in the hotel room the rest of the time. I had drinks and snacks ready when she returned, weary, at night. We swam in the pool for the few minutes she had to spare, or walked through Ottawa, pointing out places we knew. She showed me where she and David had lived for a year before having kids. Also the restaurants they'd liked. The places they'd hung out. She missed him, she said.

I had promised Paul I'd phone daily, wanting him to see that I cared for him, that my friendship with Janice was no threat to him. Janice tactfully left the room when I called.

At night we slept chastely together, comforted by each other's bodies. But there was no longer the electric tension, the indescribable caresses. It was a loss I could scarcely bear.

NINE

CRACK! A FLASH of light that was not lightning.

Crash! And the sounds of a world disintegrating. Branches hurtling to ground. A swirl of debris. More flashes of light. Unreal. Unearthly. Some kind of metaphysical apocalypse.

We woke with a start and disentangled the limbs we'd so carefully arranged — even in sleep — so we wouldn't touch breasts, hips, thighs.

It was November, and Paul was out of the country — in Africa — for a couple of weeks. Choked with dread, my first thought was: "He's come back too soon. He'll find us together in bed. He won't listen to any explanation. He'll kill us." I was sure that this spectacular disruption of the elements was my fault. My love for Janice had triggered some sort of cosmic retaliation.

She was still sleepy after her long flight. Lying there quietly. Her dark hair, which she had started to grow out, dishevelled on the pillow.

Dishevelled. That was the word he had used to describe Louise, the woman he had turned to when I'd asked for time out to consider his marriage proposal. He had begun pressing me to marry two weeks after we met, just as he had pressed — despite my saying no — for sex the first night. "I have two kids," I said. "I don't want to put them through another divorce. Just give me a week or so to consult with my analyst about this. Okay?"

He'd had an ominous look on his face that day. And when I picked him up at the airport a week later, home from a conference in New York, I was sure as soon as I saw him walk jauntily through the door towards the car, his canvas book bag slung at a cheeky angle over his shoulder, that he had slept with Louise.

"No," he said when I asked him after we got home. "I slept on the sofa in her living room. I stayed there because it was close to Columbia University. That's where the conference was. We both went."

It was not until after we'd married, after I'd decided to leave my tenured job in Montreal, after I'd committed myself and my kids to a life with him in Toronto, after I'd left my friends of ten years behind, after I'd taken out a mortgage on our pretty house in Deer Park, that he told me the truth. I was a few months pregnant with the child he feared would be ugly — even deformed — pregnant with the perfectly normal son, as it turned out, who would be the hub of our family circle — when he admitted that he had slept with Louise. She had lain, he said — dishevelled — on her bed in New York, and he couldn't resist.

I'd felt an overwhelming urge to throw up. Instead I screamed at him. An incomprehensible tirade. In response to my hysteria he pushed me onto the floor and kicked me in my rounded belly.

Dishevelled. The power of a dishevelled woman lying in bed. Now I knew that power too. Finally, I could understand.

I had wanted to leave him then. But how? I had no job in Toronto. Bea and Hugo were seven and five. I thought I had no one to turn to. My parents would just send me back. And even if they didn't, what kind of life would I have had with them and two children? I knew no one in Toronto except a few grad school friends from over a decade ago with whom I'd lost touch. To call any of them after less than a year of marriage and say, "I'm pregnant, and my husband has just beaten me up," seemed unimaginable.

The next day he had said nothing. I had said nothing. It had seemed like a nightmare. Like something that had never happened at all.

Wide awake now, I got up. Outside was the rage of an ice storm the like of which I had never, ever, seen. Through dense gusts of snow, I could see that the street was already impassable. Huge branches, weighted with white crusts of ice, were breaking and falling all along the street, dragging down with them telephone wires and eavestroughs, streetlights and traffic signs.

Suddenly, the whole city, as far as I could see in any direction, was dark. The layered sounds of fire alarms and police sirens echoed through the night. The fear and panic I felt were real. This time it was not Paul, though. She and I were alone, safe.

Janice seemed to have turned back to me, now that David had emerged from danger. For the first time we had actively conspired to plan this visit to coincide with Paul's absence. "While the cat's away, the cats will play," we had joked. Her weekend visit in November had frustrated us both. Paul had been overbearingly present the whole time. His focus had been discussions with Janice about how and when he would get her onto his SSHRC committee. Mine had been the overwhelming attraction of her smell. I realized on that visit that I could *smell* her in the house, especially in my study, where she slept. A strong, sharp-sweet, compelling scent that made me feel weak. Though neither of us said so, it was no longer enough simply to be with each other. We wanted time alone. We wanted time in bed.

Now we were both awake. I found some candles, and we sat there laughing nervously in the soft light and looked out through the whirling snow as other candles were lit in windows around us and the tracks of flashlights swept rooms in the distance. Next door a phone line dangled dangerously, spitting sparks over the driveway. I tried the phone. It was dead.

"Holy shit!" she said in the droll voice I luxuriated in. "I can't say you don't put on a show for me when I'm down east! Do you do this for all your guests?"

Eventually we grew tired again. We lay in bed kissing each other's palms. Taking turns. Licking delicately between one pair of fingers after another. Then it was those tantalizing kisses near the mouth, around the mouth, on the mouth. Kisses like no kisses a man had ever given me. Certainly not Paul. For years now, I had avoided his loose, crude kisses, turning my head instinctively to keep him from my mouth. He kissed to possess, to intrude, even to hurt. She kissed to caress, to honour, to delight. Gently I felt the shape of each of her teeth with the tip of my tongue. After a time, holding each other in defence against the night, the storm, the world, we drifted back into unconsciousness.

That four-day visit was an oasis. We both swung eagerly into this shared life, a sneak preview of the time we hoped to share later in our lives. I had never been able to count on Paul, who might drop out of social occasions on impulse or overpraise me in front of our friends (his friends, really, since we seldom saw anyone apart from his York colleagues) or berate me after we got home. Janice was deeply frustrated after years with a husband who was an introvert. David was comfortable enough with the few friends he had brought into their marriage, but shy and inept around anyone else. He believed, she told me, that it was a weakness to want the company of others.

One night we were off to dinner with a sociologist friend of mine whose feminist research interested us both. She was working not on the military/political/business history Paul's colleagues had chosen, but on a different kind of military history: the lives of women who had married military men. The next night we prepared a lamb dinner together for one of Janice's Toronto friends. She was legendary for the help and encouragement she had given women scholars who had crossed her path at the Ontario Institute for Studies in Education. These were the conversations I had long craved but seldom had.

Clearing up afterwards, Janice and I talked over ideas that had been discussed, celebrated the lives and struggles of women in academe, then went off to bed like any other couple after a social evening, to chat happily in bed and cuddle each other to sleep.

The third night — the night Paul was returning — we were off to my women's group. I had been invited to join this desultory group about eight years before after reviewing (favourably) the manuscript of the woman who organized it. The core of the group was a few of her friends from as far back as high school, but everyone was free to bring along women they thought might enjoy it. Various out-of-towners and sisters — even mothers — showed up from time to time.

From the first evening, I knew this was for me. Evenings were scheduled at random about four months apart. Food was potluck. The location rotated according to whose place was free of men for the evening. Conversations were voluble, frank and confidential. I hardly ever saw these women otherwise, apart from the one who had invited me, who became a friend. The others were figures at once shadowy and surreal to me. The qualifications they collectively held were daunting: a lawyer, a director of one of Metro Toronto's civic departments, a private school teacher in computer science, a director at a substance abuse centre, a manager of one of Toronto's mega-building-projects, three or four professors, the owner and director of a camp, a manager in one of the provincial government offices, a director at the Women's College Hospital Women's Health Clinic, an art gallery curator, a restorer of paintings and sculptures, an importer of fabrics. Yet these evenings were anything but intimidating. Dressed down in jeans, sweats, anything comfortable, this group met and drank and and talked until late into the night about anything and everything.

Almost never did they refer to husbands or lovers — though since one woman was married to the former husband of another his name came up, in good humour, from time to time. Most were not married. Only one (other than me) had children — also a non-topic. They joked and threw around ideas that in some way or other explored what was happening to women these days. How systems were changing, or not. How attitudes were in flux, and why. What strategies they'd employed to better their careers, with what success.

I had arranged one of these evenings while Janice was here. I thought she'd fit in, shine, in fact. We left early for an apartment right on the shore of the Beaches, just in case Paul arrived back from Africa before we left. I was not up to his demeaning comments about "that silly bunch of lesbians" or "those little feminist beer-drinkers."

Even though the storm had ended two days before, Lake Ontario was still in a ghostly upheaval. The beach was luminous with snow and ice, and huge foamy breakers were still cresting and thudding against an agitated tide like white ocean waves against a night sky. We parked outside the apartment and stared at this unnatural scene, waiting until we saw others go in. Between kisses we spoke quietly of how wonderful these few days had been. Perhaps it was the knowledge that we must soon leave the car, but our kisses became more and more electric. When the time came to go in, I could hardly breathe.

Janice told me later that she was taken off here and there for private conversations about me. Did she notice, she was asked, how much I had changed? They did. And they told her exactly how. They couldn't believe that I'd still used "Mrs." when I first came to their group. Nor that I was shocked to see women drinking beer out of bottles. They reminisced with incredulity about the calls to me from Henry asking for "Mrs. L." Now, they told her, I had certainly got the hang of it. They had seen me change from being submissive and conventional into an outspoken eccentric. Why, they wanted to know, was someone with so much going for her so eager to downplay her achievements? Did Janice understand me? They weren't sure they did.

When we returned, late and somewhat giddy, we found a curt note from Paul. "I've gone to a graduate student party." And with that note the whole happy mood of the last few days changed abruptly. I knew the note meant trouble. It meant, "If you go to women's parties, I'm going out to have a good time too." It was the same as Jamaica. And who knew what he would do or say next? Certainly he would be getting drunk.

I sat on Janice's bed in my study, but could not savour our time together as we had the previous nights. I was nervous, agitated, full of dread. I wanted to slip into bed with her, hold her and be held. I didn't want to talk about Paul, but I couldn't contain my distress. I went on about what this might mean. I tried to explain why his note made me "jump to," as she said. I tried to make her see how dangerous it was. I knew that if he came back and I was in there, in her room ... if he was drunk, if ... well, anything, he could become violent. She wasn't convinced. I could see she was disappointed, hurt that my attention had so quickly switched from her to him. But I couldn't risk anything. The safest thing to do was kiss her gently good night and go to bed.

It was hours later that I heard Paul's car door slam in the driveway. Hours of thinking how much I wanted her in that bed. Hours of anxiety about his return. When he noisily came in and angrily switched on the light, I pretended to be asleep.

The next day was Sunday. Since Janice was around, Paul kept his anger hidden. I suggested a trip out to Kleinberg to show Janice the McMichael Gallery. He took charge of this outing as if the idea had been his. Janice was relegated to the back seat like a child on a family outing, and Paul spoke to me as though she weren't there. He took charge of the "tour" of paintings, though he knew less about art than either of us, telling us what we ought to think of each in succession. When we came to a sculpture of a pack of wolves bringing down a deer, he observed, "That one should be called *Family Dinner*."

Along the way we ran into someone Paul knew from York. "This is my wife, Elspeth," he said by way of introduction. "And her friend, Janice." No last names. No real acknowledgment. I was, I realized, an appendage. And Janice was an appendage of an appendage.

I wanted terribly to be alone with Janice. I wanted to tell her that it was Paul, not me, who was excluding her. As we passed a women's washroom, I said to Paul, "I need to go in here for a minute." Then to her, "Coming?"

In the empty washroom we hugged each other for a long time. I said, "Sorry. There's not much I can do." She nodded. It was the only time alone we got that day.

The next morning after breakfast, Janice was dressed and ready to leave to do the research at the provincial archives that had been put off and put off because of David's surgery and long recovery, then put off and put off because of our visits. I was still in my dressing gown when Paul left for York. Drawn like magnets, we were soon on Janice's bed, whispering endearments and kissing. Eventually, I got up to shower, expecting that she would have left by the time I was finished. Instead there was a knock on the door, and she appeared, naked, to join me. We had shared showers in university locker rooms before, part of the passing parade of female flesh that only recently has stopped dressing furtively under towels or in cubicles and now strides confidently around without a shred of self-consciousness. But showering alone was different. Very different. We washed each other's backs, giggling and gurgling under the onslaught of steamy water. We each washed our own hair, and the other parts of our bodies, turning carefully so as not to touch. Then, as if by some simultaneous signal, we reached for each other and hugged. Then kissed. Still, we held our glistening, wet bodies apart, a golden arch honouring modesty.

Later, when she returned from the archives and had packed her bags, Janice sat on the living-room sofa, waiting to say goodbye. I knew something was wrong.

"I must tell you, I'm eager to get back to my family. To my husband," she said, a serious look on her face. She sat far from me, at the other end of the sofa.

"What's wrong?" I asked.

"I think we're being dishonest," she said. "I think what we're doing is dangerous. I think taking that shower together this morning was a mistake. I'm sorry. I can't take risks like that again. Paul could easily have come back and found us there. We wouldn't have heard him. I think I'd better tell you, I think he might have gone through my luggage when I was out of the room yesterday. He's sneaking around. I have unusually acute hearing, and I can hear him tiptoeing. I'm glad I'm going back today. I don't know what you're up to, Cameron, but this is too scary for me."

I looked through the big window in front of us to the street. Now the sun shone. Most of the damage from the storm had been righted. The street had been cleared. The universe was back in order. The light hurt my eyes.

"I don't know what you mean. Do you mean you're scared of Paul?"

"No, I'm scared of us. You've always said you know where to draw the line — between friendship and ... and ... something else. Something more. We've agreed we won't cross the line, that showing affection to each other, even sleeping together, is okay as long as we don't hurt anyone else. Well, where *is* the line? I think we're pretty damned close to it here, Cameron. I'm not sure there even *is* a line any more. This scares me. Things are going so much better with David now that he's recovered. I'm having a better sex life with him than I've had for years. I don't want to do anything to screw that up. Not to mention all our kids. I'm sorry if this hurts you. And I know your affection has been part of what has enabled me to get back on track with David. Your friendship has meant a very great deal to me, and I want that to continue. But I can't wait to see David tonight. I love him, Elspeth."

"I know," I said. "I'm sorry. I guess this is my fault. I understand." I was being noble. I wanted terribly to do the right thing. But what I felt was loss. Terrible loss. And jealousy. I wanted to hear those very words from her about myself. But I had no rights. And I, too, wanted to build my marriage. Her affection had given me strength to bridge the bad times with Paul. I wanted my life with him to be like the last few days with her. She had said we would live together after our husbands were gone. That was enough for me. I could be patient. I would just wait it out, even if it took decades.

Her e-mail messages took on a different tone. Mostly she was deeply engaged in a new family project. Ever since their visit to Fassiefern, she and David had talked of getting a country place themselves. Calgary was close to the mountains. She had loved the southern Alberta landscape as a child growing up in Fort Macleod. So they had been looking on weekends for a place they could enjoy in the Crowsnest Pass. Finally, in November, just before her visit to me, they had closed a deal on a miner's house in Coleman. They called it the Pass House. Out the kitchen window, she e-mailed me excitedly, you could see *both* Mount Tecumseh and Crowsnest Mountain. They had about half an acre, including a double-seater outhouse, a chicken coop that sported a picture of *The Last Supper* ("Wonder how the chickens felt about that!" she observed) and a fine stand of pine.

I could read between the e-mail lines. This was not just a holiday place, or a shrewd investment. It wasn't even, as she said, a move inspired by seeing Fassiefern. This stood for the rebuilding of their marriage. A new chapter in the McGinnis Family Narrative. She regaled me with descriptions of their shopping trips, the deals they got on furniture since Woodwards was going out of business, the difficulties of finding blinds, even the china they bought together. Blue Willow. I was devastated by this last item, for she and I had talked of the kitchen we would have when we lived together as old women. Yellow curtains, we used to say, and Blue Willow china. I had cut a picture out of a magazine and framed it in my office. A picture of a domestic room with yellow curtains blowing in the open window over a table. The room I wanted to inhabit with her. Inside and outside were reversed. The room lay beyond the window, and inside, the walls were trees and grass.

I felt more betrayed by that purchase of china than I had when Peter went off to a meeting with the woman who would later replace me as his wife. That was after I'd told him I was in labour (Hugo was born that afternoon), and I was left alone with Bea — not quite two — who followed me around with arms held up pleading mournfully, "Carra me." I felt more betrayed than I had when Paul returned from Jamaica. Yet this was a small thing. Nothing more than a set of Eaton's Special china. Blue Willow.

Their Christmas at the Pass House was idyllic, she reported. Exciting even. As a minister's daughter, she usually hated Christmas. Got the blues. Kept out of the way. Grumped around muttering, "Bah! Humbug!" But David, who really was "a little old fellow so lively and quick," loved to play Santa, trimming the tree with his boys, and crashing about out of sight to give the impression that Santa was actually there, while they waited for their presents on Christmas Eve.

My Christmas was lonely. I was at Fassiefern with Paul. It was

Peter's turn for Bea and Hugo. Henry had stayed in Barrie with his Granny and Granddad and would see us late Christmas morning for the day. Paul had asked me to knit him a sweater for Christmas. He came with me to choose the wool, a mossy green. Although I had the usual frantic duties at the end of the university's fall term, I somehow found the time to knit it. But I resented it, saw it as a test he'd posed for me. A challenge. *How much do you love me?* I kept track of the time it took — about eighty hours. His gift to me was two pairs of cheap flannel pyjamas that did not fit. I later gave them to a women's hostel.

By the time Janice returned for more research at the end of January — a visit of five days — I was resigned to making the best of my marriage. I prepared myself to give support to hers, too. Neither of us had mentioned the shower again. I understood that she had gone further with me than was comfortable for her, and she had drawn back. That, in other words, was that. I expected her e-mail conversations about the fun of the Pass House, her improved sex life, the general rejuvenation of David, to continue. They had entered a sort of midlife "nesting" phase, and the Pass House was their nest. I decided to ditch my petty jealousies, my fantasies of life with her, my need for comfort.

She had agreed to talk again to my biography class — a different set of students. I watched her grab their interest, amuse them, engage them in discussion. She was so impressive. She leaned back in the chair, just as she had at dinner in Edinburgh. It was a man's nonchalant pose, I thought. It said, *I am leaning back because I know I'm in charge. If you want to connect with me, you'll have to lean forward.* My students *were* leaning forward, paying close attention. Where had this come from? I wondered. Probably her father. She was looking quite ministerial in her tailored black pantsuit. In fact, I now noticed, she was wearing under it a black blouse with tiny white dots and a white stand-up collar. She was deliciously attractive.

As before, I could not keep my eyes from her mouth. Partly it was because she was leaning back, looking down her aquiline nose. It was a position that threw her mouth into prominence, made it the central feature of her high-cheekboned face. It was a mouth like Jane Fonda's: seriously sensual, inviting, a natural pout. I had kissed it often now. All I could think of was kissing it again, and again. We would be alone when the class was over. Alone until Henry came home from school. I hoped to God she would let me. Hoped she would not draw back from that, too.

I was not disappointed. And all my fantasies, hopes and needs came flooding back. She stripped down to her camisole and white silk knickers — an item I had never seen before, like a slip to wear under pants — and I did the same, throwing on a lace-edged cotton undershirt to keep warm. We crawled into bed and shivered in each other's arms until we were warm. I could not take my eyes off her mouth. It was like worship to kiss it. Such kisses. So expressive, so loving, so terribly passionate in the shared knowledge that "that was that." There was a line. Affection was not desire. She had made that clear. But she was not prepared to give up those kisses, that delicate tenderness, those caresses so near to the wonder of stroking newborn babies and examining intently their features for the first time.

The next day, she was off to Montreal for a meeting. The arrangement was that Paul would go ahead to Fassiefern, and Henry and I would meet Janice at the airport and drive up to meet him at the Sovereign Restaurant in Creemore for dinner. When the time came, Henry decided to go with Paul, a decision that made me ecstatic. It meant Janice and I would have the drive up to talk alone. It pleased her, too, when I met her, my heart tight as it always was when I waited for her at the airport.

The sun was setting — a cloudy red turbulence — as we drove north on the sculptured contours of Airport Road through the wintry pine farms. I could smell that familiar smell of her beside me, stronger than I remembered. She has her period, I thought. Was it possible I could *smell* that slight difference, as if it were my own body? She told me of her meeting, I chatted about my day. But gradually our conversation shifted to loving words, allusions to our hour or so in bed the day before. A silent acknowledgment — since we were both too shy to say so out loud — that we would have little time alone that weekend with Paul and Henry. That this couple of hours might be it.

It was dusk when I pulled off the road into a deserted gas station. I turned off the car and turned to her as she turned to me. Kisses on the palms, kisses on the cheeks, kisses on the neck, kisses on the mouth. Kisses of mutual need and delight. Kisses so exciting neither of us spoke at all.

When we got to the Sovereign, Paul was irritated at our being late. He had been drinking. He immediately struck up a hostile banter with Henry about women drivers. "They sure drive slow," he joked, winking ostentatiously at Henry. "Hey, we would have got here long ago. They never know the roads. They worry about ..."

Janice turned to me, ignored them, and began a conversation quietly about something else. Slowly she took off one shoe and put her foot on my ankle under the table. We were using male technology for female purposes, I thought. E-mail. Phones. Planes. Cars.

The next day, I took a cup of tea for Janice downstairs. I knocked on the door. She was awake. "Paul's just left to drop Henry at the ski hill," I said. She was wearing the same white camisole and knickers. Like an eighteenth-century wanton. Moll Flanders. Clarissa. Molly Seagrim in *Tom Jones*. "Join me?" she said.

I took off my dressing gown and slipped into bed beside her, intoxicated by her smell. I knew we had about half an hour. I propped myself up above her and slowly began those dreamy kisses we both craved. That mouth. That soft mouth. That skin, smooth waxy woman-skin. That hair, dark, dishevelled. I kissed the side of her neck, and she turned her head, moaning slightly, so I could reach almost round to her nape. To do this I had to lie across her. She moved beneath me in ways that made me clench inside. I kissed her shoulder. Kisses that moved away from her neck towards the lacy strap of her camisole. I moved it aside to kiss where it had been. She arched her back and her breast seemed to round under my lips. "Do you want me to stop?" I asked. "No ... no," she said. Slowly my kisses descended over her soft, smooth breast. The sensation was exquisite. My eager, controlled kisses. Her arching chest. The feel of that creamy breast-skin. Her breathless little moans. When I reached her nipple, broad, pale and almost flat, she whispered, "Oh ... oh." Under my lips the nipple took shape — now shrunk to something ridged, dark, urgent. I felt feverish. Dizzy. Yet I could have stopped at once, had she asked me to.

She didn't. "Sit up," she said. I rose to my knees astride her. She reached up and undid my pyjama top. I let it slide from my arms. She reached up her small hands and gently touched my breasts as if she were handling the most precious and delicate crystal. The shock of passion that went through me was unmistakable. "You look like a goddess," she said. She turned one hand away from her and slipped it slowly down my stomach and wound her fingers in my pubic hair.

I could hardly stand it. I moved to lie beside her. "Oh, God!" I said. I slid my hand down into those silk knickers, the knickers that showed her small waist and flaring, opulent hips to perfection. Silk on one side of my hand and her soft hair on the other. It was an agony of delight. I wanted to know her cleft, feel how it differed from mine. It might, I thought, be my only chance. She might suddenly draw back, decide never to do this again, as she had after the shower. She moaned, louder now, holding me to her.

"God!" I said sitting bolt upright in sudden panic. I had no idea how much time had passed. "I've got to get upstairs. Paul will expect breakfast to be ready when he gets back. Sorry." And I threw on my pyjama top and dressing gown and rushed upstairs.

As soon as I got a chance after breakfast, I said quietly to her, "Are you all right?"

"Yes," she said, "I'm more than all right. I want more."

Later that morning, Janice and I went for a walk. I sensed that Paul was on the prowl. Janice was right. He was sneaking around. Checking up on us. While we walked, I refused to hold her hand, refused even to take her arm. Sure enough, as we headed back, Paul's car glided around a bend in the road like a smooth grey shark. He waved as he passed, and we waved back.

That night Paul insisted on having sex. As usual. Unusually, though, he exaggerated his climax noisily like the fake scenes in the pornographic videos he liked. Was he doing this for Janice's benefit? She was back downstairs, and I prayed that she had fallen asleep. Hoped that she hadn't heard him. As for me, my mind was far, far away, as it often was now with him. I knew it was better to co-operate, that he would not accept no. That no, if I dared say it, would result in some form of punishment. It was easier to pretend. To move in ways I knew would end it quickly. Then he would turn over and begin to snore. Then I would feel safe.

The next day, the three of us went skiing. Paul, who was the worst skier by far, insisted on leading the way. "Look over there," he said at one point while he stopped to get his breath. "Elspeth and I saw a wolf right down there last fall. It was spectacular." "Elspeth and I ..." "Elspeth and I ..." "Elspeth and I ..." Over and over, through his comments, his gestures and the sheer space he filled even on those splayed, open hills, he asserted, *"We* are a couple. *I* own her. *You*, Janice, are a tag-along. You're lucky *we* tolerate you."

I had arranged to have dinner with Janice at my parents' on the way back. Paul and Henry were to leave about the same time to go directly to Toronto so Henry could do his homework in time for school the next day. Paul's restlessness became more and more unbearable — to him, as well as to the rest of us. Suddenly he decided to leave early. Within half an hour, he and Henry had loaded up the car and were off.

Within minutes, Janice and I were back downstairs. Back in bed. Back into the sweet world of womanly silks and skin and smells that drew us both into its delicious net like two supple fish to the lure. Now our kisses were urgent, as if we had taken up where we'd left off the day before.

"This would be easier if one of us had testosterone," I said nervously. The shyness was excruciating. It was one thing to show a man your body. Men — as Margaret Atwood wrote somewhere — would fuck hot-air registers. They always seemed to be grateful for any access to women. But it was quite another thing to expose my body to a woman. Women were more observant, more fastidious. A man wouldn't notice the odd mole, rogue hairs around the nipple, an appendix scar like mine or a Caesarean incision like hers. A woman would. How would she feel, seeing my imperfections up close? How would I feel, seeing hers?

She lay on me fully dressed, and the weight of her body, the strange feeling of breasts on breasts was exciting beyond imagination. Methodically she began taking off my clothes. Oh, God! I thought. I wish I had the body of a twenty-year-old for her. But all she could say was, "You're beautiful. So damned beautiful." She barely paused to kiss my breasts, so forceful was her need and mine. As she slid down past my breasts, past my stomach, between my open thighs, she looked up and said in an agonized voice, "I hope you realize I don't have the least idea what I'm doing."

It was over in seconds. I seized her shoulders, drew her up beside me and kissed her passionately. Then I undressed her as quickly as I could, fumbling with her clothes like a schoolboy. Her naked body was utterly gorgeous. So womanly, compared to my own straight hips and wide shoulders. She was the goddess. The very image of lush fertility. A gleaming Ceres, a soft Venus. I had no idea what to do either. I had no previous experience of this. But her tongue had given me permission. If she could take such a risk, so could I. I kissed her neck, her breasts, those extraordinary nipples, her wide abdomen, her perfect navel. I only tasted her for a few seconds when she drew me back up to her luminous face. "Did I bring you?" I asked incredulously. "Yes ... oh yes. Oh, darling."

We were already late for my mother's. We threw on our clothes and packed the car and drove off, saying nothing.

At my parents' we were shown into the living room and offered seats at opposite ends of a three-seater sofa-like piece of furniture. "Now, Janice," my mother said, challenging her as she had challenged other guests. "What do you think that piece of furniture is for?" Janice looked at it. Got up. Inspected my seat, which had a sort of chair-back against which I leaned. Observed that her seat at the other end was the same. Then puzzled over why the middle seat had no back at all. After a time, my mother, triumphant, explained, "It's a Victorian chaperone chair! The courting couple would sit where you two girls are sitting, and the chaperone would sit between them. There's no back to her seat because it wouldn't do for her to fall asleep." She laughed merrily. "Who knows what might have happened if she did!"

TEN

My PLANE ARRIVED hours before hers.

We were both giving papers at a Canadian Studies conference in Cambridge. Janice would talk about her research on women — not just Aimee, but Mary Percy Jackson, whose letters she had almost finished editing. The National Film Board were making a film and Janice was their consultant. And I would speak on the novelist Gwethalyn Graham.

We would share a room. But neither of us had been bold enough to raise the question: were we going to sleep together, or *sleep* together?

I wandered around Heathrow impatiently, plagued with fantasies of disaster. Maybe we would lose interest, prove to be unalterably hetero after all. Worse ... maybe *one* of us would lose interest. Okay. It wouldn't be me, not the way I'd felt for the two months since our abrupt separation. I faced it squarely. What if *she* lost interest. She loved David. And he was a good husband. "He leaves me alone," she had said. "Hardly notices me, actually." She'd never leave him. I could see that. Where was this all headed? What would become of me?

I could not keep my mind off her. It had been difficult to concentrate on my paper. Her feminist interest had changed my views — fundamentally. Gwethalyn Graham was a novelist whose career was — unfairly, I could now see — overshadowed by Hugh MacLennan's. She, who had won more awards and earlier than his, she, whose novels addressed the same subjects and had been translated into more languages than his, had been ahead of her time. I now saw what I hadn't before: to write a biography of someone is to immortalize him. And it had always been "him." Three times I had spent six years of my life canonizing — I now saw — male writers. Such work fixed forever the imbalances of literary history, at the expense of women. I wanted to right that balance. I wanted to rescue Gwethalyn Graham and her astonishing novels from oblivion. Problem was, there were almost no materials to work with. Mothers of girls in those days didn't save their letters home from age eleven on, as MacLennan's and Birney's mothers had done. Girls weren't expected to be famous.

As I sat in the airless lounge, across from the door Janice would come through, I noticed two young women. One, dressed in a flowered skirt and T-shirt, was embroidering a large tablecloth which she moved this way and that across her lap. The other, in cord pants and a vest, dozed, her head leaning sideways on the other's shoulder. She woke as I watched. The two of them spoke briefly, their hands touching. The tablecloth was put away. They stood up and walked slowly away. Were they a couple, I wondered? Lesbians? It was a question I never would have thought of before. I envied them their closeness, their casual touch, the way they seemed to move in a space all their own.

I loved Janice. I knew that. And I desired her. Terribly. Did that make me lesbian? Had I always *been* lesbian? Had my early experiments with my girlfriend — brief and light-hearted as they were — set my sexuality somehow?

That didn't seem possible. I had wanted men. Wanted their attention. But I had also loved them. Had desired them, passionately. And I had wanted children. A family. I could remember from far, far back that I had imagined a house with lace curtains and a white fence, and there inside, myself and four children. Where had this image come from? Was it the family I wished I had had instead of my own? I didn't think so. Was this what was meant by "social conditioning" or "social construction of gender"? Perhaps. I had grown up in that postwar decade, in the crucible of the nuclear family — an explosive social experiment, to say the least.

But now that I thought back there was no man in this image. Just me and four children. I suppose he was in the background somewhere — probably at work. But he was not real.

If anyone was stereotypically lesbian, I thought, it was Janice. She was the one with the deep voice, the crew-cut, the sailor's swagger. Strangers sometimes called her "Sir." But she seemed so feminine to me. Her body curved and soft, her skin smooth and buttery, her tiny hands gentle and loving. I was the one who was lean and muscular, aggressive and purposeful, too much for any man I'd ever been with.

Passengers began to push through the door, laden with bags and cases, the flotsam and jetsam of life in transit. I began to sweat. And there she was, striding towards me. Unmistakable in her yellow sweater and red felt fedora. The words formed uneasily: *My lover.*

Though it didn't cross my mind at the time, there was an irony in the fact that I was writing the life of Earle Birney. He was a womanizer, and for this I despised him. Esther had been unfaithful, too, but her Marxist disdain for ownership of property and people was a powerful defence. As was her knowledge that Earle had always needed other women — that he was overseas in the war, succumbing to temptation, like so many other soldiers. I was not Marxist. I believed in fidelity. Had pledged it. And meant it. There was no war.

Was I no better than Birney? Worse perhaps?

It never crossed my mind. My work seemed to be somewhere else. Neatly filed in cabinets in my office. Stored in cardboard boxes on the floor of my study. Compartmentalized, a manuscript I took out, worked on, put away.

If I had sensed the irony, I might have rationalized it. Birney had emotionless sex with many women. I sought emotional connection. Birney was in charge. I was occasionally hit, kicked or humiliated and bullied. Birney seduced women quickly. I had slid slowly into sex with the one person I had met who was deeply caring. Who recognized and liked my particular nature. Who not only was my equal but sought equality. She happened to be a woman. But I would have to have admitted that — like Birney — I was now deceitful, secretive, treading two paths at once.

THOUGH IT WAS late afternoon when we set out in our rented car, we had no idea where we would stay. We had made no bookings. We had agreed only to head north towards Cambridge and stop when we got tired. We had become accustomed to living in an unplanned limbo, emotionally and physically. It had always felt as if we were travelling with no destination, no provisions and no map. We knew how to conduct careers, marriages, children and friendships, but we had no idea how to proceed now with each other. Disoriented, anxious, but also exhilarated, we shared an adventure as challenging as setting out to find the Northwest Passage. We had to make everything up as we went along.

At Bishop's Stortford, she pulled into a gas station. "Okay, Cameron. Either you drive or you find us a place here. I'm pooped."

The Foxley Inn seemed to have been cunningly hidden. It took a long time and, finally, directions from a skinhead in black leather mowing a lawn to find it.

I got out of the car with relish. After a lifetime of waiting in cars while men booked rooms, I wanted to take charge. Janice was relieved. It had always been her job, since David was so shy. Now she could sit back and be waited on.

I knew she'd love it. It was one of those old country inns which had once tended exquisite gardens and an elegant clientele. But with the new motorway, speeding traffic between the airport and the north, it had been bypassed. Its once-lavish grounds were crowded in now by natty row houses, and its truncated gardens had slipped into senility.

Inside it was dark, and deserted, except for an inarticulate man who seemed surprised at the appearance of a prospective lodger. He led me through a dusty reading room with frayed chairs, a defunct fireplace and rows of mouldering books to the foot of a grand, circling, mahogany staircase. At its base stood a carved pulpit filled with huge sprays of pale, dusty pampas grass.

Up, then, we went, past a piano with several keys missing that stood open on the landing, like the grin of an ancient crone. Then — for no apparent reason — down some stairs, through a long narrow corridor, then up again, and round, and again up more steps to a third-floor room with peeling wallpaper and two beds: one single, one double. He threw open a door next to it to show a bathroom with a huge, stained, clawfoot tub.

"You won't believe this," I told Janice, as we unloaded our briefcases and bags in the empty circular drive.

By the time we reached the room, we had both dissolved in giggles. "Trust you, Cameron," she said. "Only you could find a place like this." She closed the door, and we both stopped laughing. "Come here."

Our kisses were urgent, hungry, fuelled by fear and the imaginings inspired by distance. We lay down on the double bed. "God!" she said. "I've wanted you."

I could not speak. Her hands knew what to do. My clothes were her clothes, too. Only a few items stood in the way — a couple of buttons here and there, shoes, not much else. I gasped for breath, could not have paused under her soft mouth, that unmistakable smell, those small deft fingers.

"God, Elspeth!" she said afterwards, lying beside me, looking right into my face and stroking damp strands of hair from my forehead as if I were a child with fever. "Men would give anything to see you like this, have you like this. Thank you."

There were no instruction books, no films, not even a clinical text to tell us what we had to learn. Even the lesbian pornography I'd seen with Paul was straight. It did not excite me. Pairs of women gyrating in gymnastic positions designed not for their pleasure but for the voyeurism of men. Gyrating had nothing to do with it. In the shy, tender experiments we conducted on each other's body before, between and after our conference sessions, we found out that less was more, that lingering kisses and delicate touch could exceed the hard pressings and graspings of men, that the glide of silky skin free of bristles and rough patches could enthral, that the slightest brushing of breast on breast could bring pure ecstasy.

I discovered something I thought of as the echo effect. That when I kissed her neck, I could feel it slightly on my own. That touching her breasts made mine respond. That her climax made me clench too. And — oddly — that I felt luxurious, completed, entirely given up to pleasure when she did.

We were, we discovered, different. I began to discover the paths she liked to follow, the rhythm of her seasons, the ways to her soul. And she explored all the routes to my pleasure, subtly different from her own. *She loves me*, I kept thinking, having to remind myself that this really was happening. *A woman loves me.* And something fell into place deep inside. A *woman* loves me. Therefore, I reasoned, I must be lovable. And from this echoed acceptance came a flood of power I'd never known before. Nothing would ever be the same again, I thought. I am changed, forever and ever. I thought of T. S. Eliot. *After such knowledge, what forgiveness?*

ONCE WE'D RETURNED from Cambridge, our e-mail swung into high gear. "I keep on having images," she wrote. "Anatomically correct images. Know what I mean? I never had a clear idea of how women are made, how I am made."

"Me, too," I'd reply. "Loving you is like loving all women, honouring them through you."

"I'm scared," she wrote. "I'm losing interest in David again —

who, God knows, hasn't much interest in me these days anyway."

"I'm doing what I can to elude Paul," I wrote. "I can hardly stand him near me now."

Two months later, she was back in Toronto, en route to an NCBHR meeting in Halifax. She had brought Leopold along. He joined Henry and Paul watching the baseball game downstairs. We sat together on her bed in my study, gazing and talking. "Listen," she said. "Someone's creeping up the stairs." Suddenly Paul appeared in the doorway, looked at us, then left.

"I'm scared," I said. "I don't think he knows anything. And he's like this, anyway. Unpredictable, intrusive. But we've got to be careful." An image formed in my mind and stayed put. An image of him walking in on us as I lifted my head like a vampire — blood dripping from my face — from her open thighs. He would kill us, I thought.

I made sure he was at his office in the morning. The boys were asleep after a night of TV movies. Only then did we make indolent love under the skylight in her room — my room.

The next day Paul didn't leave for York until after lunch. About half an hour later he unexpectedly reappeared with a potted plant, and a card that said — for no particular reason — "Thank you for making me so happy." He found us just as he'd left us, sitting on the back deck deep in discussion of Anthony Giddens, a social philosopher we'd heard speak in Cambridge, who believed in equality in love relationships — an idea we were trying to realize for ourselves.

What would have happened if he had found us in bed? I could picture the potted plant smashing, peat moss and vermiculite and tiny rosy buds all over my study, the air filled with crude insults. *Blood and blossoms on the floor.*

Her world was safer. David didn't mind us sleeping together

sometimes. She had told him we'd shared a room at Cambridge. "None of the details, of course," she wrote me. Over and over she told me that she wasn't giving me anything he wanted. And now that they had the Pass House, we could relax there in privacy.

That June, while Paul was in Africa again, I made arrangements for Henry to stay with a friend and headed west. It was late evening when Janice met me — as always — at the airport, this time with Leopold and one of his friends. In her car was a huge flat of fresh strawberries, their exciting, tangy odor permeating the night air as we drove the dark empty roads to the Crowsnest Pass.

I could not take in the little house when we arrived, could not think of anything but resting in the haven of her arms.

The next morning I woke to a sharply etched June morning, the jagged crest of Mount Tecumseh clear in the distance through the kitchen window, and off to the right the soft tiers of Crowsnest. It was enchanting. A tidy little place at the edge of town, shaded by fine rows of blue spruce and clumps of balsam poplars, it recalled fairy tales I'd loved — the house belonging to the old couple and their gingerbread man, the candy cottage found by Hansel and Gretel, the home in the forest Snow White shared with the dwarves who left each day to work the mine. This, too, had been a mining community once. And we would spend that afternoon hiking the Miner's Walk, along a frigid, tumbling stream, past banks of wildflowers and wispy ferns I'd never seen before.

But first, long before the boys woke, we breakfasted in bed on strawberries, feeding each other the plump, red fruit between lush kisses, breathing in the scent of each other's skin along with the fragrance of ripe fruit, moving from the sweet juice of berries to our own more pungent juices, feeding on each other as if at some celestial feast.

I returned to Toronto my soul glutted with love and tenderness.

When Paul returned from Africa, I invited him to lunch. I wanted to discuss the lecture trip to Germany we'd planned. I thought there'd be trouble over the hiking trip to the Pennines Janice and I intended to take beforehand. I wanted to feel safe, in a public place. Wanted to be sure he would sit still long enough to hear what I had to say. He knew Africanists there, and I knew Canadianists. Bea was in Berlin, studying for the two-year violin diploma that would augment her degree from the Cleveland Institute of Music and playing in the Radio Sinfonia Orchestra. We hadn't seen her for over two years. We could visit her for a week, and give lectures in Berlin, Hamburg and Bonn, as well.

The problem was the Pennines. Paul knew Janice and I had planned the trip for nearly two years. I had reminded him of this when we were out to dinner on Valentine's Day over a year before. Told him then that she and I had set up a joint bank account to save for it. Later, as the Berlin tour took shape, I had mentioned that I wanted to hike first, then meet him in Germany. Now I was about to make bookings. The final details had to be settled.

Over mussels and white wine at Rhodes — an elegant neighbourhood restaurant — I listened to his plans, took in the exact details of his lectures. He had arranged to be in England, too, I learned, as a consultant to a museum in Liverpool that was planning an exhibit on the slave trade. I sensed what I thought was a subtext: *Spend the time in England with me. Ditch this hiking trip with Janice.*

Instead of inquiring what he wanted me to do — as I would have in the past — I outlined my German dates, pointed out how easily they could be synchronized with his and proposed how the time with Bea could be accommodated. "That means Janice and I would leave a couple of weeks earlier," I said, as casually as I could, "and you and I could meet in the airport at Manchester to fly on to Berlin."

He was silent, pushing his mussels noisily round the dish. He took a gulp of wine, finished it, ordered more. He had a malevolent look on his face. "A couple of weeks?" he said. "This is news to me. Don't you think that's too long? You could come to Liverpool instead."

"It's *not* news to you," I said. "I've told you more than once, we've planned this for more than a year. I told you we were saving up for it. I told you we were going for a couple of weeks. Some friends of Janice's are lending us their apartment in Edinburgh." I paused. He said nothing. He was white. "Look," I added, hoping that a compromise would satisfy him, "I don't want to go to Liverpool. But I could shift some hiking days to the German trip. I'm dying to see Bea, of course. I could make the Pennines trip ten days, and meet you earlier to go to Berlin."

He threw his napkin on the table and signalled the waiter to bring the bill, leaving me to pay it. He did not speak as we walked home.

I kept calm. Held to my compromise. Made my bookings. He remained tense but did not interfere. As I later discovered, he had plans of his own.

"What? You've taken three days off our trip?" Janice e-mailed me later that day. "That means we won't have much time in Edinburgh. I'm really disappointed."

THE PENNINE WAY runs like a spine up the centre of England. Some parts are well-travelled — picturesque excursions for Sunday afternoons. Others cross over hills and through copses, or follow rivers, from one village to the next — footpaths through farmers' fields or pathways along wooded chases that have been used since the Middle Ages and before. Still others, more remote, trace routes along disintegrating walls that criss-cross bleak moors, skirting ruins that bear mute testimony to ill-fated Ice Age settlements.

We chose the older, bleaker paths. The ones layered with history, torn by vagaries of strife and climate. The ones where we could walk alone for miles, with nothing other than unaccustomed maps to guide us. The ones that lay to the north. We would find our way together along trails so faint we could never be sure we had taken the right steps. If we lost our way, we had each other. Together we would figure it out.

We happened upon Ingleton by chance. A tiny hamlet in the Yorkshire dales. That first day we were out at dawn, exhilarated by mist and drizzle. We chose paths at random, clambering up rocks, trudging along steep curving trails past puzzled sheep, slipping down damp walkways to the banks of rivers alive with violets and primroses. We passed into that other world we had imagined into being. Two girls exploring. Friends soothed by companionship. Women challenged by much to be learned — local history, quirky folklore, linguistic oddities. Janet's Foss. Giggleswick. Butter Tubs Pass. Yockenthwaite. Sharp Haw. These names that stuck like burrs to our tongues were and were not our language. Here was a waterfall, a "force," plunging into a pool where sheep were once washed, a place where witches were said to cast spells. And here a spring, a "source," believed to be the root of life. And there a moor, a "heath," a place of murders, the buried bodies of children.

We hiked almost ten hours that first day — each new vista breathtaking, each path discovered a triumph, each snatch of information a feast.

That night we fell into bed in our simple room and made love to each other as if continuing our explorations in the hills. This way ... no that ... This turn ... yes, yes ... look. How beautiful!

We made our way through deep thickets bushed with flowers and haunted by birds, along rivers of such seemly beauty they could have been lifted from illustrations for children's stories. A waterfall — perfect in form. Then another, more perfect. And another, more perfect still. A tiny bridge under which trolls might have lived. Lambs in the field round the next corner, bleating, running for reassurance, butting their mothers' udders till their hind legs lifted right off the ground.

One day we made our way up and along Hadrian's Wall, pathetic testament to the faith of man in fences, compartments, plans. Barbarians of the North (my ancestors), Keep Out. Owners of Property to the South (her ancestors), On Guard. Walls that said: Do this, not that. Be this, not that. Walls stretching from one coast to the other, the blue, blue seas on each side visible from the highest point midway.

Then Edinburgh. Our city.

Still keen to hike, to explore, to conquer, we climbed Arthur's Seat, defying the sweep of gusting winds that nearly dislodged us from the top.

And — though we could not speak much about it — we had a plan to acknowledge our bond, our union. We had joked about "marriage." Joked too about our "honeymoon." But we were serious. Silver bracelets, we had decided by e-mail. And when the day came, we walked — too fast — arm in arm to a shop in the

Royal Mile, where we had passed each other walking in opposite directions over two years before. To the clerk we were nothing more remarkable than a couple of middle-aged American tourists in Gortex jackets — mine red, hers green — and hiking boots. But choosing those two bracelets — mine an interlaced string of strong Celtic St. Magnus Crosses, hers a delicate stream of tiny silver fish — was so romantic we could scarcely speak.

Clutching our two small boxes, we walked — even faster — hand in hand, to Holyrood Castle. We slipped past a gate marked "Keep Out" and stood alone in the stone ruin of what was once Mary Queen of Scots' chapel, open now to the bleak and threatening skies above.

Janice put my bracelet around my wrist. "Forever and ever," she said.

With shaking hands, I fastened hers over her tiny hand. The fish glinted in the sun as if they were alive.

"Forever and ever."

ELEVEN

BEA AND HER GERMAN boyfriend, Alex, had chosen a lively, left-wing hangout for dinner. A smoky cave, full of students in grey or black downing beer. "Never mind, Mum," she'd said quietly out on the sidewalk after dinner. "You know how he gets. Just forget it. Don't worry. It'll be okay."

We had been speaking over our Weizen Bier and a hearty dinner about cross-cultural relationships. Hers and Alex's mainly. I remarked that Henry had a Canadian mother and an American father. "See?" Paul said loudly, so loudly that the animated chit-chat at nearby tables stopped for a moment. "My wife insults me all the time. I took out Canadian citizenship ten years ago." He turned to me with a scowl. I cringed. "Your whole family hates Americans. The first thing your mother said to me was," and here his voice hit falsetto pitch and he wagged his head as if it were a ball on a stick, "'If the Americans ever invade Canada, I'll be the first one at the border with a gun.'" Bea and Alex laughed nervously.

"All I meant was ..." I started, but he stared me down. I changed the subject. The air remained close, charged with his anger and my fear.

"Mum," Bea told me the next day when we were alone, "I think you should know this. I want to tell you why I left home at sixteen. It was him. Paul. He could never discuss anything. Never let me say anything. He couldn't stand it that I had another point of view. He would make faces and chant mean rhymes like a kid in grade four. 'Be-a's get-ting ma-ad!' That kind of thing. Once he hit me. You weren't there. Told me to get out. So I did.

"I saw the way he treated you. Remember that weekend at Fassiefern? It was horrible, Mum. It was my only weekend home that whole summer. And there I was with you and Henry and the dog in the car in the middle of the night driving off to get the police. First he was screaming at you — awful things — then he was hiding somewhere. I thought he was going to kill you, Mum. Really."

Yeah. I remembered. It was the summer of 1987. Paul had been annoyed that I wanted to work instead of going out dancing with him in Collingwood. He had grabbed the book I was reading to review for the *Globe and Mail*, a biography of Jean-Paul Sartre, and ripped pages out of it. When I followed him down the stairs, picking up the torn pages, he seized the African print I had framed for him off the wall and threw it on the floor. Shards of glass flew everywhere. He grabbed my shoulders, pushed me against the wall, thrust his face into mine and hissed, "You're a shithead. I'm going to fuck you in the ass. Right here." I ducked under his arm and ran upstairs to call the police. He grabbed the phone. The kids and I fled.

When we returned from the other direction, with the police this time, it was clear he'd expected us to come back the way we had left. He had parked the car up the road where we would not have seen it. I could see clothes hanging in it, and the duvet and pillows from our bed stuffed into the back.

Back at the cottage, it seemed he was gone. But suddenly he appeared outside the bedroom glass doors, standing in the dark on the deck. The police spoke to him in another room. Then they left.

"Anyway, when he hit me I was out of there. I just want you to know." She gave me a hug.

My stomach lurched. Tears stung the back of my eyes. A daughter lost.

"Why didn't you tell me?" I asked.

"I didn't want to ruin things. I knew you loved him. I didn't want to wreck the family."

THE BERLIN TRIP had begun badly. Paul had sauntered into the Manchester airport, his face dark as a thunderhead, forcing a grin. He noticed my bracelet at once. "Did Janice get one?" he asked.

"Yes, she did," I said, "but hers is different. Fish. We each got one," I added nervously.

"Love bracelets," he pronounced, staring at me over his coffee. I said nothing.

Bea had been polite to him, no more. She still called him Dad, a custom established when he and I had married. "Bye, Dad. Hi, Dad," she and Hugo used to say when Peter came to take them for visits. But this was a visit from me — not from us — as far as she was concerned. Now I knew why.

"Look Mum," she'd said as the S-Bahn rattled along. "See the bullet holes in that building? You won't believe my apartment." She lived in East Berlin. "It's so cool. I'm in the only place that wasn't bombed in that neighbourhood. Really. You and Dad will be staying there. I'll stay with Alex. You won't believe it. My shower is in the kitchen ... if you can call it a shower. It's only a trickle. You need a ladder to get into the bed. I have to haul coal up from the basement in winter. The stove is huge. Oh, look, Mum. There's the zoo. And there's Alexanderplatz, where the market is. Will you make us some cauliflower and cheese? I miss your cooking."

Paul was unusually restless, even for him. It was as if an electric current ran through him. He'd get up suddenly and go out somewhere. At night he was up, pacing around or rustling papers while he worked on one of the many projects he had undertaken simultaneously. When Alex was there, he seemed better. He engaged him in loud guy talk — jokes about "the girls" or mini-lectures about his work on slavery in Africa. But when he was with Bea and me, he'd walk impatiently ahead of us, or fall behind, sulking and brooding.

Bea and Alex took us to see *Rigoletto* at one of the old opera houses. Paul sat between us, shifting in his seat throughout. Even when we said our goodbyes and moved on from Berlin in our rental car, he twitched and sighed all the way along the fast-moving autobahn to Hamburg.

By the time we got there, I'd had enough. "Look," I said, when he started arranging how I was to get to his lecture and the dinner afterwards. "My lecture's in the afternoon. I think this evening I'd rather go and have a look around Hamburg." He was furious. In the past I had almost always gone to social functions with him. When he had been an administrator at York, I had hosted parties, cooked endless dinners for his colleagues, gone to more official receptions and listened to more boring after-dinner speeches than any of the other wives — even those who did not have jobs or careers. To say I preferred sightseeing on my own to his lecture and dinner was unheard of. Open rebellion.

He was asleep when I came in after a jolly evening at a Bavarian Weinfest in a nearby park. There, under gaily painted marquees, I had sampled wines, feasted on wiener schnitzel and joined in — in spirit at least, since I don't speak German — with rows of people lustily singing songs that involved standing up and clinking beer mugs at unpredictable intervals. Later, I had sat quietly and written Janice a letter.

The next day, Paul told me about everything I'd missed — the great lecture, the car tour of Hamburg a German professor had given him, the superb meal. He didn't look happy, though. When I told him of my evening, he was silent. Cheerless. Then he walked away. When he returned later, he spoke of Bonn, where he was giving a lecture the next day. He made it clear I was to come.

"No," I said firmly. "I've been thinking about it. I'll take the train instead and visit my former grad student and his wife. They have a new house in the Green Heart of Holland, and a new baby. Remember? Jon and Didy. They sent a card." He looked puzzled. "I'm not lecturing in Bonn," I added. "There's no need for me to go. My plane leaves in a couple of days from Amsterdam. You aren't flying back with me anyway. You'll be off to your meeting in Liverpool. I'll check the train times."

Jon and Didy were glad to see me. For two happy days I walked tiny Wouter in his carriage along the canals and dikes, admiring windmills and neat gardens, circumventing bicycles and the occasional billy goat. Savouring my freedom. Grand-children, I thought. I am ready. For peace. In Wouter's "Book of Wishes" I wrote: "May he have love in old age."

THE TELEPHONE WAS ringing when I got back to Toronto and walked in the door of Oriole Gardens. It was Susan, my research assistant.

"I've been trying to reach you," she said. "I wasn't sure when you got back. But I wanted you to hear this from me, not from U of T."

"What?" I said. I could tell this was serious.

"Someone broke into your office while you were away. It's okay. I mean, I don't think any of our Birney stuff was taken. Or your computer, or anything I could see. It happened when you were in England. I was there ... sort of."

"How do you mean?" I said. I felt sick. I wanted to go right down and check for myself. For a moment I felt horrified that it might have been Paul. But I realized it couldn't have been. He was away at the time.

"I was working there that evening. No one would expect me to be there at that hour, but your office gets so hot. I like work-ing at night when it's cooler. I'd just gone out for a minute, left it locked. When I came back ... around eight ... there was some-one in the office. Whoever it was had pulled the blind down. I went outside to look in. I went back to the door and called, 'Who's in there?' Whoever it was didn't say anything. I unlocked the door. I could hear movement. Someone pushed so hard against the door I couldn't open it."

It must have been a man, I thought. Susan is a big woman. Six feet, I'd guess. Young. Strong.

"I was scared out of my mind," she went on. "I got right out of there and went to the emergency phone. You know, the one near your office? Called campus police. I walked back from the other side. I figured whoever it was would get out, might leave the door open. Besides, the police were coming and that's where I'd said to meet me.

"As I came round the corner I saw a man hurrying away from the building. He went out the fire exit."

"What did he look like?"

"He had greying curly hair and he was wearing jeans and a blue shirt. He had a file under his arm. He had his back to me. I couldn't see his face. Sure looked like a professor. Anyway ... I made a full report to the police. But, honestly, I couldn't find a thing missing. And the lock was changed right away. First thing the next morning. I have the new key. I'll bring it over if you like."

"I'll drive right down to get it," I said. "Thanks. You did a great job, Susan. You must have been so scared."

When I got there I felt panic. What was the burglar after? Obviously not my computer, printer, radio or tape-recorder. Only my private files had been disturbed. I had just begun trying to trace the daughter I'd given up. I had sealed my correspondence with the B.C. Adoption Registry in a large brown envelope. It had been torn open. I felt sullied, shamed. The small legal file I had begun on my divorce had been gone through. In it had been some mysterious photos Paul had taken in Jamaica. I had come across them months after he was there when I took in the film I had used to catch street scenes of the Toronto snowstorm. There, juxtaposed with my pictures of trees laden with ice drooping over Oriole Gardens, the street completely blocked with drifts and broken branches, telephone wires crusty with frost glinting in the next day's sun, were his snaps of steamy Jamaica: shacks with clusters of men smoking — dope it looked like from the misshapen cigarettes — some kind of group excursion to what looked like a plantation in the hills. And, oddly, a close-up of a young black man, chest bared, arching back in a seductive pose, his hands up behind his head. That picture was gone. And all the negatives.

Thank God I destroyed all Janice's e-mail, I thought. I had printed out lots of it — all those letters. Five thousand letters each, we later calculated. All those months. And later, her words of love. Words I had read and reread to give myself strength, hope. Except for one or two special letters that I'd tucked into an old book review file, I had burned them all one day, fearing Paul might get hold of them somehow. I had asked her to do the same. She cried, she said, watching the papers curl, orange and black, then become smoke and dark cinders.

I had kept only the stuff she'd sent me earlier. Jokes and clippings, poems by women for women, papers she'd written. Her résumé, photos of herself in adolescence, articles she'd wanted to share, like the one on women and pornography. The only letters I'd saved were our first exchange and business ones — arrangements for lectures, our plans for the collection of biographical essays on women we were editing together, which she'd whimsically named "Great Dames." Details of our trips, maps, hiking books.

The article on women and pornography was missing. And some of the poems by women to women. Nothing else that I could be sure of.

I had photos around. Nothing odd. Pictures and cards from friends and former students. Some of Janice, David and their boys. Some of my kids, and Paul. I had a series I'd taken of the

Bench of Two Women in Mount Pleasant Cemetery, where I liked to walk. I had been toying with the idea of using one of them as a cover for "Great Dames." These had been looked through, but none taken.

I phoned Janice.

"I'm back. Guess what. Someone broke into my office, and I don't know who it was. I'm in a mess here, and I have three days before Paul gets back from Liverpool. He was horrible in Germany. Henry won't be back from camp for a couple of weeks. This is it. I'm moving out."

TWELVE

I WAS IN A WHITE fury. At myself.

I'd left personal things in my office that made me feel vulnerable now. And yet my anxiety had prompted me to destroy so much. I had got rid of the gay newspapers I'd picked up in the Toronto Women's Book Store. Curious about a side of my city I knew nothing whatever about, I had pored over their offerings: same-sex dating ads, a night life that seemed to involve leather bras or jockstraps, contests based on cross-dressing, lesbian and gay travel tours, columns on the excitements/perils of one-night stands, even ads for gay realtors, hairdressers, psychologists and palm-readers.

I was puzzled and alarmed by the photos in these magazines. It seemed that all the women looked more like men than most of the men I knew, who were not averse to flowered ties or shoulder-length hair. And all the men looked either like my own sons about age ten, scrubbed clean after their baths, or like my mother, in the veils, sequins and tulles of the fifties. Men and women alike bore knowing looks. None of the women looked like Janice or me: middle-aged professionals and mothers. I had wanted to check out the Rose Café — a women's bar — hoping Janice and I might find kindred souls there, but not enough to steel myself to go down to Parliament Street and walk in the door. The travel ads were all that really appealed to me. I could imagine the two of us hiking somewhere like the White Mountains in New Hampshire and coming back to a hot tub and videos of *Beaches, Claire of the Moon* or *Desert Hearts*, surrounded by happy women at a place that advertised itself as "Lesbian Paradise."

I also hid the only book I'd been able to find on what lesbians are supposed to *do* — a coyly illustrated number called *Sapphistry,* which was virtually no help at all since it basically said every woman is different.

Still, I had not bothered to erase from my computer a love poem I'd written Janice — an arcane, but deeply felt, tribute to the beauty of her full breasts. And my correspondence with my lawyer about the terms for divorce, and how I might protect myself legally if I sued, was on a shelf in full view.

Fuelled by rage, it took me only two days to pack up everything that was mine and get it into storage before Paul came back from Germany. Susan helped me pack boxes and boxes of things my mother had given me over the years: oriental rugs, antique silver, china, crystal and linens I had inherited from my Aunt Winnie; the many paintings and other belongings I had brought from my Montreal house. It was more than half the house's contents. The only thing I left that I considered mine was the mahogany dining table my parents had given Paul and me as a wedding gift. I carefully wrote a letter dated 7 July 1993, wishing him well in his work, referring to the break-in, and left it on the kitchen counter. I was gone.

In a state of distress and humility I moved in with my parents. Ironically, this prefaced almost two months of the happiest time I'd ever spent with them. We had more time and space than we'd ever had simply to be together. Me alone with them. No sisters. No husband. No babies. No children to distract or inhibit us from talking about things that really mattered. They had felt increasingly isolated from me by Paul, I learned. He had subtly intervened between me and them. They had talked of this often with my sisters, but not with me. How Paul always made the arrangements for visits; how Paul took the phone from me to "revise" what I'd said; how Paul used to corner my sister Lexie, who had never liked him, at New Year's Eve parties and glare at her; how Paul drank too much; how Paul dominated family conversations.

I began to realize how much my parents cared about me. I could weep openly about the loss of the family life I'd tried to build, and I received their kind words like a salve. I could speak of the baby I'd given up so long ago and hear their side of things: how my father had been so upset he had thrown up for weeks; how my mother had sensed what was wrong, but didn't know how to approach me. I could talk at last of Paul's violence, and reconsider what I might have done. They said they would gladly have taken me and the kids in when he first assaulted me all those years ago, when I was pregnant with Henry. My father — who had long ago refused to lend me $600 to repay a student loan — quietly offered me money to help with my legal expenses. I saw how deeply they meant their repeated statement: "This will always be your home. You can come here anytime."

When I told them Paul had accused me of being lesbian, they said they couldn't care less if I was. I was swept through with relief, peace and deep, deep appreciation, like a patient near death swimming up into some dim consciousness of recovery. At night I slipped into my childhood bed and fell asleep to the familiar, comforting sound of the train whistle passing through town. The same train whistle I had heard in Calgary. And in the Crowsnest Pass.

I set up my computer and worked by day on my book. Engaging myself in Birney's life was a comforting distraction. Making order of the chaos of my notes and structuring the confusion of his life felt deeply satisfying.

Within days I had managed to set up a computer link with Georgian College and mastered the complex wiring and call-in routine that enabled me to get back onto e-mail with Janice.

In late July she flew east for another NCBHR meeting, adding on several days to see me. I met her at the airport with an eagerness now marred with pain. I was free. She wasn't, and probably would not be for years. I promised myself I would never ask her to leave David — a promise I kept.

We stayed that first night at a motel near Alliston. It was hot and steamy, Ontario in July. We indulged in a naked picnic on the huge bed before devouring each other hungrily. Janice had picked up the latest *Vanity Fair* magazine and we laughed about its cover: a long-legged Cindy Crawford "shaving" k.d. lang in drag reclining in a barber's chair.

Were barriers between women breaking down everywhere? we wondered. Was our love one among many? Had women always loved other women, but were only now able to be playful and public about it? Were the suburban housewives of the fifties sharing more than morning coffee while their workaholic husbands were gone and their children in school? And what about women before that, whose husbands were overseas during the war? And before that, what about the passion for female friends before the twentieth century? There had been a sudden burst of scholarship on this subject around 1980. One historian claimed that in America during the 1700s and well into the mid-1880s, "intense friendships between women were the norm, and women were so involved with each other that men hardly figured in their emotional lives at all." And in the nineteenth century, it was common for women to sleep together, even when the husband of one of them was in the house.

The classic study was Lillian Faderman's. Her title said it all: *Surpassing the Love of Men.* Though Faderman figured that women's romantic friendships were seldom sexual, was she right? If so, would the same friendships have become sexual in a sexualized culture like ours, where gorgeous women advertised everything from banks to batteries, and the pornography industry was a multi-million-dollar business? Was it women's economic liberation over the last three decades that finally made it possible for women to choose partners freely, without having to depend on a man's income or face poverty? Or had the sexual revolution of the sixties freed homosexuality just as it had freed sexual language and situations? Leon Edel had rewritten his biography of Henry James to include the homoerotic content he'd known about all along. Movie ratings now warned of "sexual content" and "coarse language," but the very existence of such scenes was quite recent. Such content and such language had been what made foreign films so enticingly racy only a decade or so ago.

Which of these speculations — or what combination of them

— could account for what had happened to us?

We had no idea. But as our reading expanded and we noticed things — like the greater physical closeness of models in fashion magazines and the appearance of gay characters in TV sitcoms — we began to speculate that many, many women might have found and loved each other in the past. Many more probably than the 10 percent of the population most serious writers on the subject claimed were gay. As Janice often commented, society was set up in such a way as to encourage women to display themselves and compete for men. There were plenty of fences in place to keep women from women. But women bought magazines full of women, just as men did. Fashion models — not photos of men — engaged their imaginations. And as I often commented, wasn't a baby's first love and bonding with the mother, whether the baby was male or female? Maybe the deep sense of intimacy and comfort we both felt came from some rediscovery of that bond.

Separately — she with David, me with my parents — we watched the BBC serial on the love affair between Vita Sackville-West and Violet Trefusis, "Portrait of a Marriage." Together, after she flew east again, we watched the new 1993 release from the National Film Board's women's branch, Studio "D": *Forbidden Love: The Unashamed Stories of Lesbian Lives.* From it we learned of the terrible fallout for Canadian lesbians in the fifties — raids on women's bars, indignities, invasions of privacy — and witnessed the courage, integrity and humour of those women, often married, who had chosen each other. We watched erotic scenes — based on old lesbian pulp paperbacks with titles like *Daughters of the Devil* or *Girls' Dormitory* — in a daze, over and over again. It was just how we felt: those delicate advances and retreats; that gut-wrenching shyness; that unmistakable lust.

But it wasn't research and brainwork that kept us together. It was an attraction so complete, so profound, so magnetic that we felt like soulmates. Like twins separated at birth who had accidentally encountered each other and at once sensed an emotional affinity. We expressed that attraction, that encounter, that affinity now with our bodies, adoring and pleasuring each other, but sex was only one of a thousand languages in which we communicated delight.

We spent two days with my parents in Barrie. They returned to the phrases they had used long ago when my sisters and I were at home. "Are you girls ready for a drink?" my father would ask. Or my mother would say as we came in the door, "I suppose you girls would like a nap?" Yes ... yes.

"We want to have a midnight dip," I announced one sultry evening. And Janice and I drove out to their friends' cottage on the lake, stripped off our clothes in the moonlight and slid into the delicious cool water, our breasts buoyant between us. Two mythic water nymphs, sleek and white in the dark lake.

We left for Toronto and Janice's meeting in a flood of rain. By the time we got to my office to work together for the morning on "Great Dames," we were soaked through. I turned on my fan and we draped most of our clothes over chairs and set our shoes in front of it. There, we happily spent the morning in our underwear, working hard.

I joined Janice at the end of the day at the Chestnut Hotel after her meeting. The shyness and defences that had inhibited us before had partly fallen away, and, although we intended to work a bit more, the mere sight of each other half-clad in underwear or dressing gowns was enough to excite us to make love over and over, seized with a passion I had never before experienced. We were like animals in heat.

I returned to Barrie and e-mail in a daze. I counted every day until Henry returned from his camp and we boarded the plane west. Originally the visit had included Paul, but, like the summer before, it was only Henry and I who took the plane.

Meanwhile, I found a small, funky apartment in the student ghetto west of the university and, with the help of my mother and my sister's teenaged stepdaughter, moved in my furniture and clothes.

It should have been a relief. The end of life with Paul.

But it was not.

Suddenly I developed terrible anxieties.

The first panic attack hit out of nowhere. I thought I was having a heart attack or suffocating from something toxic. Or maybe it was some extreme symptom of menopause. I was sweating, felt faint, short of breath for about half an hour. But it was not simply physical. I was filled with dread.

The full horror of what I was doing crashed in on me. I would lose my friends. My home. Maybe my children. Paul might stalk me, kill me. I would never have Janice. Or, if I did, it would not be for years and years.

I wanted only one thing clearly.

To die.

THIRTEEN

THE PANIC ATTACKS would not stop. They got worse. Now I was panicking at the very thought that I might have another attack. I could think of nothing but suicide. I had detailed plans. A train? Too brutal. Hanging? Uncertain about my knot-tying skills. The balcony of the Park Plaza? A horrible thing to do to passers-by. A truck? Same problem. Sleeping pills? How would I get hold of enough? A trip to the U.S. to buy a gun? No idea how to go about it.

I stopped eating entirely and my weight plunged. I could not eat, forced myself to down bananas and milk whipped smooth in the blender. Everything about my apartment seemed ugly: the smell of cat pee by the front door, the rotting wood on the little deck, the filth on the window sills, the way the cupboard doors didn't fit. I scrubbed and repaired obsessively, but new tasks seemed to come at me and at me and at me like rain in a hurricane.

I felt as if I had been skinned alive. Like a rabbit hanging in a butcher shop. As if whatever divided me from the world had been torn away, leaving nothing but raw nerves, exposed innards. The slightest breeze or touch might sear me or prick me into intolerable pain.

I downed beta-blockers and tranquillizers but could not sleep. Hour after hour I lay in bed, wide-eyed, terror seizing me at whim, twisting me into sweats and shivers. Day after day I moved further and further into a repulsive nightmare I was powerless to stop. I needed my home. I needed Henry.

One night my youngest sister phoned. She talked to me for hours, for what seemed like the whole night. "You must not go back to him," she pleaded. "He'll kill you. You know I've never liked him. But I thought from the moment I met him that he might be violent. Like a bad dog. One that can't be fixed. He's dangerous. You know that. I know that. If you feel that bad, for God's sake go to your doctor and get some Prozac. It really works for acute depression. That's what's wrong, I think. Please, please, don't go back. Look ... I love you," she said, for the first time.

And her words were something to hold on to.

I returned to my old therapist. The one who knew about the violence. I asked for Prozac. He prescribed something similar. "It will take six weeks to kick in," he said. I forced myself to recall my sister's words. Forced myself to think of every single person who would be hurt by my death. Hoped I could make it.

My visits to the therapist were oases in a desert.

"Phone him," he urged. "Call Paul. Tell him you want to come back."

Paul agreed to meet me in Queen's Park. He looked different.

His face had a look I'd seen on the faces of old men in Times Square, where I'd once sat waiting while he checked out the porn places. The look of some kind of addict. Skin taut. Unsatisfied. Exhausted.

His narrow blue eyes were transparent, intense when he spoke. We sat on a park bench and he lay down with his head in my lap. I stroked his hair back from his forehead. Passers-by glanced at us.

He began in a whiny voice to talk of his childhood. Of how little he'd been given. Of his mother's electric-shock treatments in the mental institution where his father had had her confined because she was schizophrenic. Of how he'd recently visited two cousins in the States he'd never met before. Of what beautiful women they were. He pulled two photos out of his pocket. I was shocked. One was very plain, heavy and vulgar looking. The other looked garish and cheap: bleached hair, too much make-up, artificially thin. This, I realized, was his idea of beauty. I swore I would stop bleaching my hair, tone down my make-up and — if by some miracle my appetite returned — never, ever, diet again.

We met a few days later in a shopping mall. We agreed I would cancel my apartment lease and move back in Thanksgiving weekend. After only two months, I was going back.

As soon as I got back into my house, back with Henry, I felt better. My appetite gradually returned. In a week I could sleep. Somehow, somewhere, I believed that Paul had learned his lesson, that he had had time to think about what it meant to lose me. To lose the continuity of our life together, the family we had both wanted to build. I thought he would change.

What had changed was me.

Paul began pressuring me at once for "wild sex." What he wanted was anal intercourse, to stick huge plastic vibrators and other objects in me, to make me lie in the bathtub while he peed on me. I had put an end to this before, but I'd always felt guilty about not satisfying him. Now I found it easy to say no. "I want tenderness, cuddling, gentleness," I told him. He wasn't interested.

When he came home one day with a $700 snowboard for Hugo's Christmas present and asked me to pay my share, I easily refused. He had been able to get me to pay half his legal bills over the assault charge, but now I was sure I had no obligation to share the cost of a gift I had not chosen, a gift I thought far too extravagant. I calmly said so. When the Blue Jays won the World Series for the second time, and he assumed I would rush out with him into the crowded streets, I had no trouble saying I didn't want to. "I don't like hysterical crowds," I told him. "There's a good chance people will get hurt."

I went through my closet and threw out all the clothes I felt uncomfortable in: the leather miniskirt, the elastic red minidress that stretched just enough to cover me, the crotchless underpants he'd given me, the low-cut sweaters, the black lace pantyhose, the high heels that hurt my feet.

Paul was furious.

"Fine," I said. "Let's discuss this."

I invited him to stop pacing and sit down.

"The way I see it," I said, "you want me to wear these clothes that make me look like a slut." He nodded.

"Well, I don't want to look like that. I'm fifty. I'm a professor. I don't want to try to look as if I'm twenty. I'm hardly prudish, but these clothes make me feel uncomfortable. And high heels are painful. I won't wear them any more."

His face looked threatening. "You'll wear them," he said. "I'll get you more. You'll change your mind. I know you."

"While we're on the subject," I went on slowly, "you have told me often that you don't want me to buy clothes for you, not even as gifts. Right?" He looked surly and confused. "You won't tolerate any comments from me about your hair. I've heard your friends tell you you need a haircut. You don't get mad at them. I've lived through beards, moustaches, short hair, Afro hair, shoulder-length hair, hair braided with beads, ponytails. And I have seldom said a word. I can't remember the last time I did. So why do you think you have the right to tell me what to wear? Why do you expect me to maintain long, bleached hair and painted fingernails? Why do you feel entitled to choose my clothing when we go out? This is a double standard, and I won't go along with it any more. I will decide what I wear and how I do my hair. You keep out of it."

He stormed from the room. My heart felt like a steam pump. Then I felt hungry.

THOUGH I COULDN'T have put it into words, all that remained was Henry. Paul had never hit either of the boys. Only me. And Bea. But I was afraid for him. Afraid that if I weren't there, Paul would have no other target.

It was late November and Paul was putting up the Christmas tree. Henry was helping. They had left the front door open, and I became alarmed that the kitten Henry and I had recently got might have escaped. Out I went around the block, calling and searching for her. When I came back, Paul hurried outside and pushed me up against the wall. "I'm glad your cat has disappeared, you bitch," he hissed, his face thrust right into mine. I began to cry.

"What's going on?" Henry called out the door. Paul released me, and we went back into the house. "Sit down, you two," Henry said firmly. "Now, Dad, what's your prob?"

Paul puffed himself up and pressed his fingers together in an inverted 'V.' "Your mother is abusing us," he said. "She's mad at us for leaving the door open."

"Okay," said Henry, turning to me. "What's your prob, Mum?"

"I'm just upset that we may have lost Puzzim," I said. "I'd like the two of you to help me look for her. It doesn't help to have Paul say he's glad she's lost."

"You did say that, Dad. I heard you. I think you owe Mum an apology. I'll go upstairs and check the cupboards. She might be in there.... Here she is," he called down a few minutes later. "I found her."

Paul never apologized.

It was shortly after that that Paul flew into one of his tempers and stamped upstairs. "I'll go talk to him," Henry said. "I can handle him. You're right, he has a terrible temper. But he cools off fast, too."

Paul did not cool off. I could hear them talking upstairs, Paul shouting. He rushed down the stairs and out the front door. Henry went after him. "Dad, you come back in here. That doesn't solve anything. Come in here and sit down. Mum's right here waiting for you to talk about it. Come on."

As the two of them came in the door, I saw that Henry was a bigger man than his father.

WHEN JANICE'S LETTER arrived that fall, a response to my e-mail telling her that I'd gone back, I did not open it. It was thick, and typed on university stationery.

I had a good idea what might be in it. I could not bear to read of her pain, her anger, her betrayal. Nothing she could have written would have outdone my self-recriminations. But I knew that reading her words, imagining her voice, might whirl me back into panic, might put me over the edge. I could scarcely face my classes that September, was trembling all the time.

"Please keep messages neutral," I e-mailed. "I don't want to become one of the women you speak of so bitterly, the ones you gave to, the ones you say fed off you and gave nothing back. I want to keep in touch. But please keep it neutral ... for now, anyway."

Our e-mail shrank to almost nothing. Mainly it was business arrangements over "Great Dames." She cancelled both the trips to Toronto she had planned for that fall. I expected her to back out of our co-editing project, but she didn't. Though her messages were curt and brusque, she did not cut me off altogether.

In the two months I was gone, Paul had expanded into my study. After a week or so, I had asked him to move his papers and books. He did nothing. One day I decided to collect his stuff and pile it on his desk. Under some Visa bills was a set of negatives. I held them up to the light. They were mostly photos of a woman. Some were of Paul. I could make out our kitchen in some of them. Others, I thought, were at Fassiefern. I had them developed. Yes, I was right. There was a tiny Asian woman with heavy make-up and long black hair posing in front of our sink and perched — cheesecake-style — on the kitchen counter. And there she was again — in jeans and the kind of open, loose blouse Paul liked — sitting demurely at what must have been a lunch at Fassiefern. A bowl of fruit. A bottle of wine. Another shot of Paul at the head of the same table. And one of each of them in the field outside the house, "Miss Saigon" (as I immediately dubbed her) holding a bunch of wildflowers.

Long ago I would have felt jealous. Now I felt chilled. This middle-aged woman was trying desperately to look young. She seemed a reflection of my own worst fears. I, too, had clung to long, dyed hair, make-up, diets, to please Paul. Had I looked this bad? This sad? Looking more closely I could see that "Miss Saigon" had dressed to disguise a potbelly. The thick make-up made her look older. The prim white stockings she wore in the kitchen poses were at odds with her jaded face.

I decided to say nothing. I put the negatives with the other stuff on Paul's desk.

Janice could not avoid her NCBHR meeting in mid-December. She would be staying, she e-mailed me, at the Chelsea Inn. I invited her for lunch, and carefully wrapped a movie guide book as a Christmas gift, after inscribing it "To the McGinnis Family."

My chest was tight as I saw her stride up to the table in my favourite Greek restaurant. Despite the cold outside, it was possible to believe you were in a sun-drenched *taverna* on the Mediterranean. I felt disoriented. She was wearing a new navy pantsuit — her "gangster suit," she called it — and her hair was permed into tiny brown ringlets that fell below her ears. She had lost weight — a lot of weight. I knew what that meant. The last few months had been as hard on her as they had been on me. She walked right up to me and kissed the side of my neck. Then she sat next to me, not at the place set opposite. Her knee touched mine. I could hardly speak, her vivid presence and the familiar smell of her perfumed skin excited me so.

Lunch was awkward. She was angry. Despite her brave show of warmth, she was as remote as a vine twisting high and away on a rooftop. I could sense tendrils reaching out, but they were not for me. She would not discuss Paul, she said. Nor did she want any information about my personal life. She would not speak of David, or their private life, either. We spoke of "Great Dames" a bit. She told me how difficult her fall had been. How wonderful her friends had been to her, helping her through a terrible time of grief. She was over it now, she said. *Over me,* I thought. Certainly she seemed cheerful. I tried to explain, without mentioning Paul directly, that I, too, was stronger, better. She commented that I had put on weight, and I explained my new resolve never to diet again. "I feel stronger than I have in years. I'm so grateful for all you did for me." I could not yet tell her how close to death I'd been. How the images of my own death had almost tempted me to act. That she had saved my life.

She had gifts for me, too. Books, I could tell from their shape — one for Christmas, one for my birthday. We agreed to a second lunch a day or so later.

We met at the Arcadian Court, where Aunt Winnie had often taken me. It wasn't much changed, the huge art deco restaurant floor like the ballrooms on the sort of cruise ship she used to love. I felt safe there. Beside the restaurant was a new art gallery. I suggested that we look in after lunch.

Janice seemed even more angry than before. She spoke again of her wonderful friends in Calgary. This time she was more pointed. She made it clear that they had come through for her, whereas I had "dropped her on her head." She wanted to know directly what I expected by way of a relationship with her now.

I was flustered. How could I convince her that I was changed, transformed? Something had happened inside that had made me a different person. Things with Paul were also changed — perhaps because of this, perhaps because of "Miss Saigon," whose sudden appearance eased my guilt. It wasn't so much that I had decided not to cringe around him, not to do anything I didn't want to do or that I didn't think was right. I had changed so essentially that I could act only as I did. I would not accommodate him any more because I could not do so. That meant in bed, too. He and I had been having talks about sex. I said he had no idea about me physically, that I had been nothing but a prop all these years, not much more than one of those life-size plastic blow-up dolls. He said that all I wanted was cuddling and "stupid stuff like that," while he wanted "wild sex." We were, he said, incompatible. "I want you to be my sex slave," he said.

Since I had moved back in, he had not worn his wedding ring.

How, I thought, can I answer Janice, when I have no clear idea who I have become? How can we discuss this when talking about Paul is off-limits? What, exactly, is she asking anyway?

"I want our relationship to go on as it has," I managed. This was wishy-washy, I knew.

She looked astonished. She wasn't going to leave it at that. "You mean the physical part too?" she asked.

"Yes," I said. "I think so."

I could see from her face that she did not agree with me. I felt a tightness in my chest. Tears threatened. This was it, then. I interpreted her face, her questions, her tone of voice to mean that our relationship had shifted into something like friendship, maybe mere acquaintanceship. I was, I thought, to be one among many friends. And the better friends were those near her, the ones who helped her instead of draining her, as I had.

We looked at the paintings next door, commenting on them without humour, not touching hands, shoulders, as we would have before. Then we took the elevator down to the parking garage and parted at the car. She took my arm and drew me to her. "I love you," she said like a neutral statement of fact. She kissed me then, chastely, on the mouth. This would be the last time I would ever hear those words, feel that mouth on mine. I was sure.

CHRISTMAS WAS STRAINED. Janice, I knew, would be at the Pass House — another chapter for the McGinnis Family Narrative.

Henry wanted to stay with my parents. Paul wanted to have me to himself at Fassiefern. We would drive over Christmas morning to open presents and celebrate Christmas dinner. My parents had agreed to tolerate Paul, but they did so on condition that he not be there for the big family party at New Year's. My sisters had refused to be in the same room with him, my mother said. Nor would she or my father, now that they knew how he'd treated me, were it not for my pleas that they support my effort to save the marriage.

Christmas morning I asked Paul to come skating with me on the pond at Fassiefern. It had turned cold and clear, and the ice had snapped frozen before the snow fell. The pale clear panorama of rounded hills was so inviting. He refused. So I skated alone on the pond in the early Christmas light while he worked on one of his many African projects indoors.

It was that morning I knew it was over. I felt a complete dissociation of his interests and mine — what I saw as his inability to have fun, enjoy being outside, enjoy *anything* other than work and sex. He saw me as wasting time, wanting to do sporty things he was no good at, ignoring the Great Africanist at my side.

It was at dinner back in Toronto after that difficult Christmas that Henry asked if we could go to Granny's for the New Year's *ceilidh*. He loved their *ceilidhs*, wanted to see his aunts and uncles and play with his younger cousin. I told him no, not this year. Why? he wanted to know. Paul said nothing. I had not told either of them about my mother's request. We were there for Christmas, I said. New Year's was the only time his aunts and uncles could visit. They saw Granny and Granddad much less often than we did.

Paul turned to Henry and pushed his chair back from the table. "What your mother is saying is that they don't want me around. That's why we're not going." He was shouting. He left the table abruptly, his meal half eaten.

"It's true," I said to Henry. "They all want to see you and me, but they're angry at your dad."

"Why?"

"They know now about the violence."

He nodded.

As soon as Paul could book a flight to Africa, he was gone. The day after New Year's. He'd be away, he said, a couple of weeks.

I knew something was wrong when my birthday came and went and I heard nothing from him. When he walked through the door, he greeted Henry warmly, but he did not say anything to me. He didn't even look at me.

When we were alone, he said, "I'm moving out. My feelings are dead. You ruined this marriage, Elspeth. You've ruined my chances at any further administrative jobs at York. Unfortunately, you have a thing about the police."

I felt nothing but relief.

He did not, however, leave. He set up a bed in the living room and slept there for two nights. Finally I asked him when he intended to go. He seemed unsure. "Look," I said, "you said you were leaving ... so go." That night he was gone. Henry told me he had moved up to Fassiefern.

With Janice almost completely out of the picture and Paul gone, I threw myself into finishing my Birney biography. On the side, I worked with my lawyer to get the divorce underway. At first Paul wrote me on e-mail, trying, he said, to arrange an amicable settlement. But his e-mail became more and more bizarre, more and more accusatory. I was, he wrote, a neglectful, abusive mother, a despicable wife, a poor scholar ... the list went on and on. Also, I was financially irresponsible, cheap, did much less than he did at home. He accused me of "harassing" his mother because, when she called me about our separation, I told her for the first time that Paul had been violent. And he hinted that he could tell my father about my lesbianism and show them documents in his possession to prove it. When it came down to the details of settlement, he was vague, inconsistent. His idea of an amicable settlement seemed to be one in which he called all the shots. "I'm going to have it all," he told me on the phone. "Our house, Fassiefern, Henry, everything." I stopped sending e-mail.

My lawyer and I drew up an offer in March and delivered it directly to Fassiefern and to his office. I accepted that this would be a long, expensive process, possibly one that went to court.

I was feeling strong in ways I had never before felt strong, content on my own with Henry, who relaxed into a busy life of hockey and friends that overlapped occasionally with mine.

Suddenly, Janice e-mailed that she would be in Toronto in April for another meeting. I had not told her that Paul had moved out. I knew it was a final separation, but I knew she wouldn't believe that.

"Come and stay with me and Henry," I told her. She declined, saying she would not go near Paul again. "Paul isn't here any more," I said. "He moved out a couple of months ago. I'd like you to stay here."

She agreed.

FOURTEEN

"I WANT TO MAKE one thing clear," Janice said when she saw me in April. "I don't want you out here this summer, lying around our house like you did the last two."

I could hardly blame her. That April visit was strained, though that didn't stop us from making love as passionately as ever.

Now we were on two entirely different tracks. She was still married, still committed to the McGinnis Family Narrative, still deeply engaged with setting up the Pass House. They would spend most of the summer there, she told me. She'd managed to get David interested in hiking. But I was definitely separated now. Heading towards divorce. I was free.

It was a heady time for me. Like being set down somewhere I'd never seen before, with no maps, no compass — just wilderness to explore. Freedom was mine, mine for the first time in my life. I had rapidly moved from home to university residence to pregnancy in Vancouver — a married woman at nineteen. Three years and two university degrees later, I was living with Peter in San Francisco. Then married to him as soon as we'd both divorced. I had lived alone for almost three years before I met Paul, but "alone" meant two little children, an exhausting round of illnesses, play-schools, birthday parties and a series of live-in *au pair* girls to be trained, accommodated, mothered. I had entirely missed out on the independent stage of life that follows childhood. I had never really lived alone.

Even now, there was Henry. But he was almost fifteen. He preferred to make most of his own meals and eat them in front of his favourite TV shows, often with friends. His weekends were sacrosanct — no place for me. Mysterious plans were hatched by phone minutes before their execution. He'd hang up the phone and be off until his midnight curfew. I was more alone than I'd ever been before. Free to choose what I wanted to do, with whom, when and where.

In July, with Henry back at the camp he loved, I led a writing workshop in non-fiction at the University of New Brunswick in Fredericton. I lived again in residence, on the campus I remembered well from my grad school days. For two glorious, summery weeks, I took part in a literary community of fiction writers, poets and children's authors. All my students, it turned out, were women. We joked and played, worked and worried, criticized and supported each other. Those daily workshops in a little stone one-room building, the casually shared cafeteria meals and experimental evening readings or plays confirmed a love of life I hadn't felt since I was a child.

Soon after that, I left for Siena, Italy. I had enrolled in a summer course on Italian frescoes. I knew nothing about frescoes, had never studied art history, but the thought of five weeks in Tuscany, travelling from there to churches and official buildings and galleries with works by artists I'd scarcely heard of — Giotto, Lorenzetti, Fra Angelico, Masaccio — sounded wonderfully exotic.

By the time I left for Siena, I was too excited to be much perplexed by the fact that, since I'd left Toronto, I had not heard at all from Janice.

She had wanted my addresses, and had promised, as she put it, to send me "letters that I could keep under my pillow." I had written to her a couple of times from Fredericton — on one occasion using a card with two old ladies such as we might become, in hats and gloves ordering lunch at a European outdoor restaurant — and I sent off another letter from Berlin, where I stopped over to visit Bea. I wrote again on the train as it rolled past the orderly farms of south Germany and down through dark tunnels until it burst into the golden landscapes of Tuscany and finally ground to a stop in Florence. I expected to find a letter at the front desk of the residence, but though many of my fellow students from Toronto were happily seizing on waiting letters from home, there was nothing for me.

Nothing for days. Nothing for three long weeks. Then, when a letter finally showed up in my box, it was short and almost cruelly friendly. Nothing of love, nothing of missing me. Certainly nothing to put under my pillow. Only cool accounts of family outings, trips to the Pass House, lunches with friends, swims at the university pool. She signed it "Love, J." That was it.

I was puzzled, disappointed, but not devastated. I was enjoying my summer far too much for that. But I took careful stock. What did this absence of letters mean? Had her clear discouragement of any plan I might have had to spend the summer in

Calgary with her been more serious than I thought at the time? I could see she wouldn't want another summer tending to me, even if I weren't in some state of distress. But had she really decided she wanted me out of her life altogether? She had been very enthusiastic about my plans for Fredericton and Siena. I had assumed she was just happy to see that I *could* get on with my life in an independent way. But was there something she wasn't telling me? Had her affair with me turned out to be merely the catalyst that improved and strengthened her marriage to David?

I hoped not. But how could I know? I could not fathom why the one letter she had sent was so distant. I decided not to change my behaviour on mere speculation. I loved her. I felt passionately about her. I would write these things to her, no matter what she wrote — or didn't write — back.

Perhaps it was the distance, or perhaps it was that the Italian frescoes and the terra-cotta towers of Siena engaged me so deeply. But her behaviour did not knock me off balance. I really *had* got myself a life — for the summer at least. I began painting water-colours again — something I'd hoped to take up at Fassiefern — trekking to picturesque sites with another student in the course and sharing the paints she had brought along. After the summer, I would return to my classes at U of T. I was lucky, I figured. I had my home, my job, my son, my family and my friends — good friends who supported me and would not see Paul. Having tasted freedom and independence, I would continue to make decisions that seemed good to me.

One of the things I needed to figure out was whether or not I was — in a phrase from *Forbidden Love* we had joked about — "like *that*." Was I lesbian? Or had I just fallen in love with a person called Janice, and gender hadn't seemed to matter? Alone much of the time during days off, weekends and out-of-class time, I mulled these things over. If I *was* lesbian, I thought, and if Janice *was* picking up her marriage again and wanted to keep me at a distance, how would I conduct the rest of my life?

I argued to myself that I had always wanted a husband, children, a family. But what had marriage done for me? Not much. No one had ever treated me as badly as Paul. Peter was simply cold. And Mark and I had been too young, an undergrad couple who, as social mores loosened just a few years later, would simply have lived together while we went to school.

Sex with Janice was actually the first really loving sex I had had in my life.

No, I thought. No. I have not always been "like *that*." I had loved men. Had I been loved tenderly by men, I would have stayed with men. Now it was too late. I could never trust any man again.

From now on, my life — sexual or celibate — would be with women.

In the American bookstore in Siena I found the Penguin collection of lesbian short stories. It was a large collection, but I finished it none the wiser. Some women seemed to know very early that they were lesbian. Others were but didn't know it. Still others weren't but somehow crossed a bridge as I had, late in life. I was just confused.

All I knew was that I wanted Janice.

I needed a clearer idea of how she felt.

E-mail, I thought. Surely there is e-mail somewhere in Siena. And there was.

It took two weeks and complicated negotiations in the stagnant summer heat with an Italian instructor in the program, but finally, he got me a password and printed out the long, detailed instructions I needed to get onto the Internet at the University of Siena. The computer building was far from the residence, and it was open only at odd hours. The few computers they had were in a small, crowded room on the sixth floor. But every day — usually twice a day — I walked the steep narrow streets of Siena and climbed those six flights of stairs in temperatures of thirty-plus degrees. At the top I would wait, sweating and out of breath, until a computer was free, then send off a message.

For a few days there was no reply.

Then came back: "Typical, Cameron. I should have figured you'd get yourself on e-mail ANYWHERE." She sounded annoyed. As if I had intruded. Sent messages that were unwelcome. Her messages were still the letters of nineteenth-century ladies ("Today I took lunch with my dear friend so-and-so. It was most pleasant. The children are both fine. Etc., etc."). Gone were the glimpses of passion, the eagerness for my words, the playful innuendoes, the intellectual discussions, the longing to be together. I still didn't know what to make of it. But I did what felt right to me. And what felt right to me was sending steady messages and letters telling her how happy I was. How much I loved Siena, Assisi, San Gimignano, Padua, Florence. Loved the frescoes, my painting, my freedom. Telling her how much I missed her.

Even if I could have nothing else, I wanted her friendship. I would phone her as soon as I got back, I promised on e-mail. I couldn't wait to hear her deep, rich voice again.

It was the first thing I did when I walked in the door.

FIFTEEN

I WANTED TO DEDICATE my Birney biography to her. But how? I could hardly say "For the woman I love ..." or "To Janice, without whom I could not have written this book because I would be dead." I settled finally on "For Janice Dickin McGinnis, from whom I learned to appreciate the West." It was a pallid compromise. But it was true, it was apropos since Birney was a westerner, and to her it would imply much more. I hoped when she read it she would see something like "For Janice, from whom I learned to appreciate the West — and women, myself and life."

"Yeah," she drawled when she read it. "Appreciate the West ... and a few other things, Cameron."

She flew in for the book launch, an elegant reception at the Principal's house just beside my office at University College. She had bought a pale-yellow suit with a short skirt for the occasion.

I could not take my eyes off her. It was — I now see — a harbinger of later transformations. Now it was I who wore the pantsuit, though it was beige silk. And it was she who was the more feminine, her wide flared hips and small waist accentuated. I was the one with the boyish bob. Her thick chestnut hair had grown almost to her shoulders.

I had invited family and a few close friends back to the house for turkey and a salad afterwards. When everyone finally left, she and I donned terrycloth robes, hunkered down in our chairs like two teenagers at a pyjama party and indulged in a post-mortem while we gnawed in shameless greed at the turkey bones, throwing the remains into a soup pot we'd put on the table.

High on intimacy and wine, we abandoned the dishes and headed upstairs, where she told me how terribly proud of me she was. She made the sweetest imaginable love to me in a silence too precious to be broken by words.

The next day she was gone.

NOVEMBER WAS A problem. She was to spend the month in Toronto giving lectures for the university's Canadian Studies program, an arrangement that had been an on-again, off-again thing ever since I'd first conceived it a year or more before. At first it had been understood she'd stay with me. Then, when I'd gone back to Paul, she'd decided to stay at the University Women's Club. And now, though I was free, she held to her plan. She said she thought it would be better that way. She could visit on weekends, and I could come to her room sometimes (I could scarcely imagine ever *leaving* her room). She said she would enjoy having an independent base. I suspected she was too stubborn to change a plan she had made because of my indecision.

Or that she didn't want to admit that she'd like to live with me.

Back and forth we went on e-mail. Me pleading with her to stay with me. She arguing the merits of separate quarters. It boiled down to Henry. "You don't want him to know we're lovers," she said, "and that means I'll have to sleep in a separate room anyway." It was a direct challenge. Where did I stand? What was most important to me?

It took hours of thought, endless lists of pros and cons, vacillations back and forth, before I decided that what was important to me was that month with Janice. I wanted to share ordinary days in ordinary ways with her. Henry, I reasoned, would be okay. We hugged each other every day and I told him often how much I loved him. He and I had had over a year together, and I knew he was well settled in school and busy with his friends. I had no intention of flaunting anything, but I felt sure he could handle whatever he observed. He had spoken easily to me about homosexuality for years, ever since he shocked me when he was about ten by clumsily telling me a joke about some rock singer being weighed down by semen in his stomach. What harm could result from being around so much love?

"We'll sleep together if you come here," I finally wrote her, "and I will answer honestly any questions Henry asks."

I felt no fear and no shame.

That November was extraordinarily fine. Even late in the month we enjoyed impromptu picnics in the Mount Pleasant Cemetery in front of the sculptured Bench of Two Women, who reached out towards each other. I photographed them over and over from every possible angle. How many women, I wondered, separated by space, custom or fear, had silently longed for a woman's touch they could never have and turned their hearts to stone?

Every morning we let Henry practise driving on his way to school and then took the car down to our offices at the college. After the day's work, we would go home like any other working couple to shop and cook dinner. While Henry watched sitcoms, we escaped the canned laughter to outings around the city: movies, walks, theatre, ballet. One warm night I surprised Janice with a picnic of roast lamb and Greek salad, a small flask of scotch and fresh bread on the Toronto Islands. On a deserted late-afternoon beach we leaned against a huge piece of driftwood and watched the light fade into the blue hour. "No one," she said in disbelief, "has ever done such wonderful things for me. It's always been my job to organize the family, make the decisions, arrange the food. I love the way you decide to do something like this, and then just go ahead and do it. God, I love you, Cameron."

At night we lay around in pyjamas, reading newspapers or books, and Henry would wander into the bedroom and chat with us about his doings or play with his cats. The three of us had chosen a new kitten from the litter next door and had named her Miss Ogilvy, after Radclyffe Hall's short-story character. After Henry had wandered out again, leaving Miss Ogilvy to bed down in Janice's fragrant hair, I closed the door and we made passionate love to each other. With such an expanse of days before us, we had time to experiment with each other, to refine what we already knew of the delicate delights of each other's bodies. Sometimes, after delivering Henry to school, we would both be so overcome with lust that we would return home to spend the morning in bed, lying afterwards in each other's arms as if floating in a world of myth.

"Jesus, Cameron," she would say, "whoever would have thought sex could be so good. I mean there's *no* comparison, is there?"

"Don't you feel there's something missing?" I would joke, quoting a line from a Jeanette Winterson story I had read in my ongoing research on lesbian doings.

"Yeah," she would say. "And I'm glad it is. The penis is completely redundant. When you make love to me it is all about me. And when I make love to you it is all about you. There's none of this worry about pleasing someone else while trying to take your own pleasure. It's so ... so ... luxurious."

As the month neared an end we began to talk tentatively about what it all meant. One evening as we got dinner ready, we stood in front of the stove, keeping warm as the night cooled. We were to go to *Swan Lake* that night.

"I always identified with the prince," she said as we anticipated the performance. "I wanted to wear those great velvet jackets, and pants tucked into leather boots. I never identified with the princess. I wanted to *rescue* the princess, free her from the tower, help her get a life." She laughed.

I didn't laugh. "Look," I said, apprehensive already about her departure only days ahead. "What are we going to do? I mean, with our lives? It's been wonderful ... this month together. What are we going to do?"

She stopped laughing. "Yeah," she said. "I can't see doing anything until Anatol is out of high school. That's a good five years from now. I guess we'll just carry on as we have."

"Look," I repeated, awkward with emotion, propping the oven door open so the heat would warm my cold back. "I've been here alone with Henry for over a year now. He's always busy with friends. We seldom even eat together. I have no adult here to talk to, to share things with. For over a year now, you and I have come and gone — your place, mine — but there is a fundamental difference. When you go home, you go home to David. You have a partner. Even though I know you and David haven't had sex for months, you have companionship. You and I hardly ever get to see each other. Henry will be finished high school in two years. What do you expect from me?"

Her face tightened. I couldn't read her expression.

"I want you to wait for me ... however long that takes," she said quietly.

I felt panic building in my chest. My voice changed to a thin whine. I could hear it but was helpless to do anything about it.

"I think I could wait until Henry goes to university. That's another two years. But Anatol will be three years after that. By then I'll be fifty-seven. And then what? Maybe by then you and David will have worked something out for yourselves." Again it occurred to me that maybe I had been used as a catalyst to revive their failing marriage. Not deliberately, but still ...

I felt desperate.

She shook her head, but said nothing. I could feel the tears sting. Feel my face twist. God, even two years seemed forever. I wanted to live with her. Now. Right away. Carry on as we had all through November. The delights of her mind, her humour and companionship all day, the comfort and pleasure of her body all night. I couldn't stay there in the kitchen. I fled from my feelings to the dark bedroom. Dinner was out of the question.

Eventually she came upstairs. "Come on," she said gently. "Let's go to the ballet. You'll feel better." She had nothing more to say about the future. I was devastated. The ballet seemed as remote as one of Saturn's moons. She closed the door on my weeping.

When the final day came, I could hardly say goodbye. The night before I had cried and cried in her arms. The last time we made love was an acrid mix of ecstasy and pain. Now, before leaving for my office, I gave her a cool hug and left her packing her clothes, sure she was happy to be going home.

I checked my e-mail compulsively. Five hours later she was there.

> They've all been fine. Busy. When I asked the kids if they missed me they said no. I've had a running conversation with D. about how little we think of each other when apart (or together for that matter). I have a feeling that I have changed fundamentally and that they have as well. What a wonderful month. I'll be back anon after I unpack. Forever and ever. Love, J.

Henry never asked about anything.

SIXTEEN

"THERE'S SOMETHING I must tell you."

My therapist — formerly our marriage counsellor — looks expectant. I had returned to her to try to find out what the hell had gone wrong in my marriage. To understand. She sits silent.

I can't speak. I can't get it out. Five minutes pass ... maybe ten. It is a risk involving nauseating fear. She's heard Paul accuse me of being lesbian. She's heard my denials. Now I must tell her and take the consequences. It's too important not to. It is a waste of her time and mine to conceal the question that consumes every thought: What will become of Janice and me? Still I can't speak. I am sweating the cold, sharp sweat of terror.

"I ... want to tell you about ..." I am determined to tell her, but I can't do it. I just can't do it. "I am in love," I state baldly.

"Yes?" She knows this is not all. She waits, silent.

"It's ... it's ... a woman," I say. I sound so foolish. So at fault. She waits. "It's ... it's Janice," I blurt out.

My turn to wait now, catapulted into a horrible limbo. What will she say? Will she turn on me disapprovingly? Will she loathe me? Will all the respect and care she's shown me disappear, leaving me not only without Janice but comfortless, a therapist's pariah?

I feel as if I will suffocate.

She looks right at me. "I'm not surprised," she says. "I felt it might be something like that." *Will she damn me to hell?* I am mentally poised for flight from her office, from intense distress. "It's wonderful," she says in a quiet voice. "Wonderful. You deserve to be loved. Tell me all about it."

So began the first of many conversations through December that led to the risk I never thought I'd take.

"What do *you* want?"

"I want to live with her."

"What's stopping you?"

"Her. She loves her husband, her boys. I don't blame her. David is kind. He's not at all like Paul. He knows we sleep together. Not the details, just that we share a bed sometimes. He doesn't ask, and he doesn't mind."

"Have you asked her?"

"Asked her what?"

"To live with you."

"No. I couldn't do that. I don't want to pressure her."

"Okay, so what's your bottom line?"

"Well, the longest I think I can go without seeing her is a month — maybe six weeks." I pause. She waits. "You mean I should tell her that? Try to work it out?"

"What do you gain by saying nothing?"

"That way I don't force her to say no. I can have some of her, even if it's not enough."

"What would be so awful if she did say no?"

I began to cry. "I want her so. I mean ... I want to live with her. If I can't live with her, I need to see her every month at least."

"What would you do if she said no? If she called you today and said she can't see you again? What would you do?"

I try to take in the question. I know it is *the* question. Tears keep coming and coming and coming. I say nothing. I try to think about it. What if that worst of all possible scenarios occurred? What *would* I do? I don't think I could bear it.

It took several sessions to figure this out. Rather, it took several sessions even to face the possibility.

What *would* I do?

Not suicide, that much was clear. I felt strong. I felt like a good person. I felt true to myself. Being loved by a woman had given me the deepest approval I had ever felt. Janice's love had helped me love myself. To love her had been to accept all women as lovable, including me. And the therapist's gentle acceptance of my choice, of what I had chosen as a new sexuality, gave me hope and confidence.

What would I do?

I would live comfortably alone — despite the loneliness I knew I'd feel. I would grieve for my loss. No one could replace Janice, I knew that. We had discovered this other love together. We had given birth to one another. We had broken through some barrier together into another world. It had been like waking with a third eye that sees what most others never see. A brave, new world of the heart. We had composed something beautiful and enduring — like a triumphal hymn with lilting themes, unexpected harmonies, exquisite reverberations. The coda too could be a thing of beauty.

Eventually, I would seek and perhaps find another woman to love. I was sure I could not love a man again. Could not allow men — with their rough bodies, their crude imaginations, their dangerous needs, their alien souls — close to me again. But I might find someone else, someone different from Janice. Someone whose love I could bask in in another way. At fifty-three I couldn't count on it. But inside I felt it could happen. That I had a good chance of finding what I needed, and part of what I needed was someone to give to.

I decided to get things clear with Janice. I knew the risk was that pushing now might end everything. Forever and ever. My model was my friend the painter Doris McCarthy, whose memoirs I had long ago reviewed. I admired her integrity in ending an affair with a married man when it became clear he would not leave his wife. She had managed to keep his friendship afterwards and to say nothing. Even in her recollection, she refrained from naming him.

"Darling, this is going to be a fairly serious message, so brace yourself," I e-mailed in mid December.

> I have been thinking about David. About how unfair this situation is to him. You and I have full information to work from. He doesn't. I'm not any longer comfortable with that. I am feeling apprehensive about coming there in January as planned. I cannot just enter your house as you entered mine in November. It's not just that I can't sleep with you (a major point), but that I am automatically the outsider. The "couple" is you and D. I am the mistress. I've been here before. I recognize the feelings:

exclusion, degradation, confusion. I tend to rationalize and adapt. I want to raise the possibility of telling D.: you, me, or both of us.

I have also been thinking about a remark you made: that you despair of having enough to give me. I think this is a serious problem. I love you terribly. When you left I missed you more than ever before. The more time I spend with you, the deeper my feelings go. The deeper my feelings, the more committed to you I feel. The more committed I feel, the more hurt I am when you go home. I am in danger of drawing back on the one hand, or of becoming masochistic on the other.

Right now I feel a 100 percent commitment to you as my partner. You say you don't want to make a choice. But you HAVE made a choice. You have chosen the status quo. I don't mean this is good for you. You too show the strain. And given the fine person you are, you must be troubled too. You have said you are.

Wait for you, however long that takes? I don't see this as controlling, or even as a request. Just your wish. We must realize that my waiting might well be in vain, were I to do it. And how would I feel if I DID wait — say for ten years. Would I be resentful and angry? Would you respect me? Would YOU be willing to wait if the situation were reversed?

Deceiving D. or anyone else offers me nothing. I feel no shame, either in relation to family or friends.

You on the other hand say that your feelings for D. run as deep as those you have for me. (What you actually wrote was, "This man has been a partner of mine for over twenty years. We have built good lives together and produced good children. I do not know what the future holds, as I said, but I know I will always feel connected to this man, even after separation and death. My feelings for him have some of the same depth as my feelings for you.") This is chilling for me, Janice. In person you have told me things at odds with this — e.g., that you have never felt as connected to anyone as you do to me, that D. was always off in his own world, etc., etc., etc. You'll know what I mean. It's as if you are appealing to me to put up with having so little of your time because D. is so nice. Sorry. I believe there is something hollow about your marriage. Maybe the real point is your revised statement that you DID love D., not that you DO love him. You seem to make a case that you chose a good father and husband — in that order. That the job of childrearing is almost ended. That the father role is pretty much all that's left now. You feel a responsibility to keep up a fairly conventional (your words) façade. This is called an affair, Janice. This is called keeping a mistress (gender of course irrelevant). If I see your point, I'm expected to put my needs and wishes aside so you can fulfil a responsibility to a man you no longer love, who has not indicated he feels the same responsibility towards you. I'm not willing to put my needs and wishes aside for this reason. Sharing a good deal of your life is what I propose. And less than a quarter of your time is not enough for me. Forever and ever. E.

Having started on this route there was no turning back. I offered choices that were acceptable to me. She would not choose.

Because my plane was late, she wrote, she had told David that she would spend that night with me in their guest room. I said no. "Either I sleep with you during my visit or I use the guest room entirely," I wrote. She spoke vaguely of "evolution" and of "making everyone happy" and of how it would be "abusive to D. to tell him." She decided I'd have the guest room.

I pressed further. "What I feel is disrespect for my behaviour and yours," I wrote.

All I can control is my behaviour. If we are talking many years — and you say a minimum of five, while I say two — I don't think I can continue to be hurt as I am each time you go home. You say "I'm not giving you anything D. wants" and "D. lets me do whatever I want." Okay. So I propose we spend summers, Christmas holidays, other holidays together as a couple. During the teaching year, you live with your family. If you decline, I want to forgo the intimate part of our relationship for the time being. This would make me feel better about myself, and about you. It would be a risk, of course. I might meet someone else and find the intimacy without strings attached that I want. You might also find someone (a woman probably) with whom you found the physical intimacy that is lacking in your marriage. Or you might revive that aspect of your marriage.

If we were to take this path — of limiting ourselves to a professional partnership and a friendship — there would be still a possibility of getting together in the future on equal terms. I am making you a proposal for partnership now. You see, I love you, but I love myself too and am going to protect and look after myself this time round, no matter what the outcome. E.

SEVENTEEN

IT LOOKED LIKE THE end of what we called JE. JaniceElspeth. A unit. Soulmates.

Janice informed me matter-of-factly that she and her guys were making a Christmas trip. They were going to have their traditional Christmas Eve at the Pass House a day early. David would dress up as Santa, as usual, dispensing presents. Then they would drive on to visit David's relatives in Portland, Oregon. It would be a great chance for their sons to bond with David's relatives, she wrote me. What I interpreted this to mean was that Janice herself was consolidating the McGinnis family. Yet another chapter in the McGinnis Family Narrative, a chapter that clearly excluded me. I asked if I could phone on Christmas Day. Not possible, she e-mailed. They would be on the road.

I knew this plan was Janice's, not David's. He never spoke of his relatives, whereas she talked often of hers — of how mean and stubborn the Clarkes were, how off-the-wall funny the Bartletts, how taciturn the Dickins. Anatol was a Bartlett, she used to say. Leopold was like her — part Clarke, but mostly Bartlett. I knew David had almost no contact with his two sisters (his parents were both long gone). I imagined this trip as Janice's bid to make David feel important. It would be *his* family for once.

I could almost hear her building bridges: who resembled whom, who had inherited which character traits, what possibilities there might be for future visits so the boys could get to know their father's family better — for the first time, really.

The beginning of the end.

I arranged to have all three of my children for Christmas. Bea and her new boyfriend Peter would fly in from England. Hugo could take a train from Montreal. I also invited my sister from Ottawa and her husband. Together, we would go to Barrie to spend Christmas Day with my parents. I knew the hustle and bustle would keep thoughts of Janice at bay — a little, anyway.

Even so, I felt loss and grief. I had made a proposal and got several things clear, despite her evasiveness. Her response had been to ask me to pose no more "hard questions" and then retreat deeper into her family. I had little if any hope of commitment from her side, and decided for my own well-being to cancel the trip to Calgary in late January. I would explain when she got back after New Year's.

It was in this frame of mind that I decided at last to check out the Rose Café, a bar and dance spot for women. I knew my future was with the lesbian community. I wanted no one but Janice, but if she simply moved me back into friendship and recast our affair as an unwise fling, I would have to get on with my life without her. I needed to brace myself by checking out what this community was like. I had no intention of anything other than observation.

It took every resource I had to get myself there one slushy evening just before everyone arrived for Christmas. I phoned the day before to gather whatever information I could.

"Is this a bar just for women?" I asked, my heart gripped with apprehension. "Yes," answered a woman whose voice was non-committal.

"When does it get busy?"

"People stop in for drinks anytime after seven o'clock or so."

I thanked her and hung up quickly.

Next day I drove past the place to see exactly where it was.

In spite of my elaborate preparations, when the time came, I could hardly force myself through the door. It was dark inside, and it took my eyes a minute to adjust. Disappointment was immediate. I had expected a cheery group of women at tables or standing at a bar. Music probably. But the place was almost deserted, except for a small group of men and women who were chatting as if at a cocktail party. I sat down at the empty bar. Exposed. Uncomfortable. The woman tending bar asked me what I'd like. She didn't seem lesbian to me — I mean, I never would have thought so meeting her anywhere else. I ordered a draft beer.

I felt duped. Where were the women who supposedly dropped in for drinks? What were all these men doing here? Well, I was in here now. I would stick it out. I braced myself in case I met one of my students, or someone else I knew. I felt exposed. A reluctant exhibit in ... what?

I looked around. The place was divided into two levels. At one end was a disc jockey's booth, uninhabited for the moment. Soft non-stop mechanical disco thumped through ceiling loudspeakers wrapped with Christmas baubles. Near the booth a large TV displayed Madonna in a Wonder Woman bra and not much else, strutting to music that could not be heard. At the other end of the room on a raised floor were a few tables with chairs. A couple of women played pool in a desultory fashion. In between was an empty dance floor backed by a huge wall-size mirror. Nothing, I thought, could induce me to dance in such a setting.

One of the men from the cocktail group came over and sat on the bar stool next to me. He looked like a frog. I looked away.

"Wanna dance?" he said, taking a long drink from his glass.

I ignored him.

"Wanna dance?" he said, more loudly this time.

I looked right at him. "No thanks," I said.

"Ah, c'mon. Wanna dance?"

I felt anger surge up into my throat.

"No," I said. "What are you doing here anyway? This is a women's place."

"It's our Christmas party," he slurred, leaning towards me and grinning his frog grin. His eyes bulged like Peter Lorre's. I noticed he was wearing a wedding ring.

"Is your wife here?" I asked.

He looked startled, then confused. "Uh ... no."

"Why not?" I said.

"She doesn't like these office parties. C'mon, wanna dance?"

"No," I said, feeling like a vindictive missionary. "What do you think you're doing asking *anyone* to dance. You're married. Go home to your wife, if she can stand you." And, surprised by my self-righteous tone and the vehemence with which I had spoken, I left the bar stool, leaving the frog man opening and closing his mouth as if gasping for air.

On the edge of the dance floor where I now stood were a couple of young women — about the age of my students — chatting. They had drifted in with a few other women who now began to greet each other, hugging and kissing and talking in an animated way.

"The guy at the bar is bugging me," I said, in a panic. "Can I join you for a few minutes until he gets lost?"

"Sure, no problem," they said in stereo, looking me over curiously. I did not look like one of them at all. My tailored pants and jacket seemed somehow out of place. The shorter one was wearing a baseball hat backwards over a dark ponytail. She was tiny, elf-like. Had she been bigger, she would have looked like a baseball player on his day off: sloppy sweatshirt, sleeves pushed up, over battered jeans. The other, a large, plump girl with a pink baby face surrounded by light ringlets, wore a frilly blouse and loose pants. They didn't seem like a couple, but how would I know?

They wanted to know who I was. Why I was there.

I said I was a teacher, hoping they wouldn't ask where or of what. People immediately clam up on learning I am an English professor. Mostly they make some excuse about their poor grammar or inability to write so much as a postcard. Did I have a partner? they wanted to know.

"Yes," I said, "but she lives in Calgary."

"Oh, God. Long-distance relationships are the pits," one of them said. "I got into one of those once. You can't trust anyone at that distance."

"Tell me about this place," I said.

The large one said, "Well, you have to be careful. Looks like you're new here." I nodded. "See that one at the bar — her and the one beside her?" She glanced at a woman in her forties wearing a leather jacket and jeans, and another beside her in a fringed jacket and pants and boots. "Like, don't *ever* get alone with those two, either one of them."

"What do you mean? Any woman has to be better than some of the men I've been involved with. My husband was violent."

They laughed. The little one twirled round impishly on one foot, then bent double. "You think *lesbians* are any better?" she said when she straightened up. "I tell you, those two could chew nails and spit rust. You'd better be careful. *Real* careful.

"Say, where do you teach?" she asked after a moment.

Here we go, I thought. "U of T," I said, in a tone of voice that implied it was some sort of junior high or community college.

"You do!" The little one was delighted. "Maybe you know my dad. He teaches there too. What department are you in?"

"English, but it's a huge institution. I'm sure I —"

"*English!* No way! That's my dad's department," she said, naming a colleague I knew well.

I felt ill. But before she could pursue this any further, the disc jockey arrived and began a loud spiel welcoming all the "ladies and ladies" to the Rose Café. Her words were soon drowned out in the deafening beat of disco. Women seemed to pour in now from the street: couples I recognized as butch and femme — the butches like tough motorcycle guys, the femmes in miniskirts and thigh-high stockings. Paul would have liked them, I thought. There were other couples I recognized from my readings as "Bobbsey queers" — girls with exactly the same clothes, haircuts, shoes, even jewellery. But mostly there were women of all ages in pants and shirts and no make-up. Women I would never notice as anything other than the secretaries, business women, professionals or whatever they were by day.

My two young friends pulled me between them onto the now-crowded dance floor. "Dance with us," they laughed. And I did, moving in that crowd of women as if caught in some Dionysian rite. Suddenly, a couple of women broke from the pulsating mass and clambered up on two tiny platforms at either side of the dance floor. One was a stocky leather dyke with hair cut like James Dean who stomped and slicked her hair back. The other was a sinuous black girl in a tiny miniskirt and stretch halter top who undulated as if in a spastic trance.

I avoided using the washroom. Once it had been a refuge from men. Now it could be dangerous. I knew men had washroom sex — did women, too? What if I got stuck in there with one of the two dykes at the bar? After a few beers and a couple of hours of dancing, I'd had enough. I thanked the two young women, grateful to escape before my new friend offered to say hello to her dad for me. As I pushed my way through what was now a crowd of women at the doorway, I found myself face to face with one of my graduate students. "Hi," we both said, astonished. "I'm just getting out of here," I said awkwardly and hurried past her into the cold, damp street outside.

I wasn't sure what I'd learned from my night at the Rose Café. I was confused. This community didn't feel comfortable to me. It hadn't seemed much different from hetero bars. It was pleasant to see couples of women dancing together, talking affectionately, holding hands and gazing at each other as Janice and I had done. But it still felt dangerous, out of control somehow. A smoky flesh market with trance-inducing music. The kind of music that gives permission. It seemed to have nothing much to do with the deep soul connection I felt with Janice, nor with the life of embroidery, reading, gentle stroking and intimate loving we had so often imagined for ourselves.

In the car on the way home I heard a song that somehow captured the terrible melancholy I felt. I listened carefully for the singer and song afterwards. Suzy Boggs, "What Have I Got to Do to Make You Love Me." The next day I got the CD and played it over and over and over. Yes, it was a sad, sad situation. I played this song and cried and cried whenever I was alone.

Grieving had begun.

CHRISTMAS WAS OTHERWISE dampened. One after another we came down with a gut-wrenching, feverish flu. My turn was last. After everyone had gone except Hugo, it hit me full force. I was in bed in a fitful achy sleep when Hugo called me to the phone.

"It's Janice, Mum. I told her you were sick and sleeping, but she said it was urgent. Sorry to wake you ..."

Janice? It was two days early. She wasn't due back until the fourth, the third at the earliest. I had fixed on the fourth to protect myself from disappointment. I was restraining myself from checking my e-mail until the fourth. I took the phone.

"Darling," she said. "Are you okay? Hugo said you're sick."

"Yeah," I said, befuddled with headache and fever and sleep. "Just the flu. You aren't supposed to be back yet, are you?"

"Nope. We hit some bad weather and changed our plans. I missed you. I can't wait to see you."

"Look," I said firmly. I had prepared this as my first speech to her. "Look, I won't be coming out there this month. I just can't visit casually any more. Sorry."

"Darling, I thought you'd say that. But listen. I've done a lot of thinking over the holiday. I can't accept your proposal. It would be too hard for me to have a double life."

It was what I'd expected. I just wanted to go back to bed.

Nurse my flu. She went on, but I hardly heard her.

"I've decided to live with you, if you'll have me. If not, I'll live alone. I've told David I'm leaving him. That was important to me. To tell him before discussing it with you. I've told him I'm leaving whether you'll have me or not. I'm doing this for me."

Then silence.

"You see," she went on, "I saw this movie. You know, with Geena Davis? From *Thelma and Louise*?"

She paused. I couldn't take it in. A movie? *Thelma and Louise?* Told David? Living with me?

"Hey, *say* something, Cameron. I'm telling you I can't accept your offer, because I want more. I want the works. *Say* something, dammit!"

"I'm sick. I can't take this in. You want *what*?"

"You, babe. JE. Life together. I'm leaving David no matter what, anyway. What do you say?"

"I don't know what to say. Have you actually left?"

"No ... David and I have worked it all out. We aren't going to tell the kids until later. We want to pick a time that doesn't disrupt their school. After exams, I guess. I figure I can leave by May."

"May?" I was stunned. May? I counted out the months. Five. Could we really be living together in five months?

"Why? What made you decide?"

"I told you. It was this movie. We saw it over the holiday. *Speechless.*"

"Sorry, I just can't think what to say."

"No ... no, that's the *movie. Speechless.*"

I had never heard her talk this fast, sound this enthusiastic.

"You see, the Geena Davis character is engaged to this one guy — he's played by Christopher Reeve — and this *other* guy falls in love with her. Michael Keaton. Christ, the Reeve guy has been with her for two years and he not only doesn't know her, he doesn't even *try* to know her ... and the *other* guy gets her number right away and really respects her, really connects. See?"

She paused.

"No ... I don't get it. But you can tell me later. I'll go see it myself. So what's going on here? You mean you're leaving David? For good? Seriously?"

"Yes ... oh, darling, yes. Isn't it wonderful?"

I was ... speechless.

"Well ... *say* something, Cameron. For God's sake. I need to hear something, anything."

"Well ... that's wonderful," I managed to get out in my fluey voice.

I was scared.

"I want you," she said, serious now. "Really want you. I want years and years. I want to go places with you and see things and read things and talk and talk and talk. And hold you and be held. To wake with you beside me and know we have that day and the next and the next after that. To feed you and be fed. To sit at Stratford holding your hand — or in theatres or trains or beside fountains."

"Yes," I said. "Yes."

"But I want us to think carefully about how to do this," she went on. She was miles ahead of me on a trail of her own choosing. "Try to make it as easy as possible on the people affected. Our kids, David. Everyone. I need to keep talking to David about this. Work it out together. Choose the best time to tell your guys. Our parents. At the end of this term we can be together. We can go to that lighthouse in P.E.I. you said you can rent. Oh, God! I love you so."

She paused.

Finally she said, "You know what David said when I told him? He sat there and thought for a while. Then he said, 'I'm going to miss your soups.' That was it. That was all he said."

EIGHTEEN

COULD A HIKING TRIP on Kilimanjaro or Everest have been worked out with any more caution and precision? Like any major expedition, telling family and friends about JE was planned in meticulous detail.

We did not know where or how we were going to live. The coming year was my sabbatical. I had planned to leave Toronto no matter what, knowing what happened to professors who are glimpsed collecting their campus mail or are encountered at parties of colleagues. Their advice is sought. They find themselves on "just this one" committee. Graduate students phone to ask for "this special last-minute letter of reference." I had spent all my other sabbaticals and leaves looking after kids and supporting husbands' careers. This might be my last year off to do research and write. I intended to use it for myself.

Paul was dragging his heels on our divorce. But I would not let his delays ruin my sabbatical year. I would wriggle off the hook. I'd have to be available for examinations for discovery or a pre-trial or trial, but if I didn't leave Canada, that could be worked out. He had ignored my second offer to settle, but he might suddenly speed up and push for settlement. As always, the only thing I could expect from him was the unexpected.

He had not been around most of the time over the year Henry and I had lived at home. Much of the time he'd been doing research in Africa, leaving no forwarding address or phone number for his lawyer or even for Henry. By the time my sabbatical began, I would have lived with Henry alone for fifteen months.

My first talk was with Henry. Already he'd complained that he hardly saw his father. Months before, I had suggested he ask for a week or two with him. He came to me in tears shortly after to say Paul had told him he couldn't afford it. That was absurd, I thought, but did not say so. A salary of almost $100,000? Fassiefern such a cheap place to live? All his expenses in Africa covered by grants?

I began after that to broach the subject of my sabbatical. Henry did not want to leave Toronto. He wanted to stay in the same school, spend time with his friends. I invited him to suggest options along with mine. Why not close off the stairs to the basement, he said, and let Paul live downstairs while I lived upstairs? That way he could go back and forth between the two of us. I recognized the painful fantasy of all divorced children: to bring their parents back together. Gently I explained that I could not live in close quarters with a man who had hit me. Henry, who unfortunately had seen some of Paul's tempestuous outbursts, understood.

Between us we came up with a plan that suited us both. I

would leave Toronto for my sabbatical, and Paul would move into the house and support Henry for the next fifteen months. Henry wanted lots of phone calls and visits from me, but otherwise was happy at the prospect of "cooking with Dad in the kitchen." Because I had seen him stand up to Paul, I did not fear for him.

Now the e-mail flew back and forth. The decision with Henry cleared the way for other plans. I would spend my sabbatical in Calgary. This meant we would have to find a place to rent. I flew out in March to check out apartments with Janice. Up and down the streets we went, noting For Rent signs and following up newspaper ads. There were so many places available, at rents so much less than Toronto's, I was delighted. Janice wanted good light, preferably southwest. I wanted enough space to write. We needed a place for kids to stay over. She knew the city, which districts would be best.

It wasn't until we saw a tiny blue bungalow with a garden for sale that the thought of buying crossed our minds. This little house with its sunny rooms and quiet location looked like a home — could be *our* home.

It would hinge on David, Janice concluded. He wanted their Calgary house and wanted the boys to stay on with him. She was to have the Pass House. But if he would agree to sign for a second mortgage, there might be enough money for a down payment. The money we would be paying for rent could cover mortgage payments instead, even though I would be paying half the mortgage, insurance and taxes to maintain my equity in the two Ontario properties until my divorce was settled.

"I'm sure David's *glad* I'm leaving," Janice kept saying. "He seems so happy. He's eager to help us out with a down payment. We'll have to figure the details, but I think it will work.

Honestly, it seems like he's getting what he wants. He told me that all along he's been planning his retirement a year from now without me in the picture. Makes me angry. I wish he'd been up-front about his feelings. He must have switched off long ago. I mean, the man's shared a bed with me for over a year now without ever laying a hand on me."

The bungalow, we decided, was a money pit. We had both been through renovations. Never again, we agreed. But now that we'd figured out how to buy instead of rent, our search for a home broadened. As I returned on the plane to Toronto, round in my mind swirled the condo with the balcony, the house with the patio, the townhouse with built-in everything, the New-York-style loft with the raised bedroom in the historic ware-house. But there was nothing I really wanted to own.

I didn't pay much attention to Janice's e-mail describing a wonderful townhouse with really interesting spaces. I was too busy ending my teaching term. I booked another flight to Calgary, hoping that this time we would find a place we both liked enough to buy.

We had agreed to tell our kids about us at roughly the same time. Janice had decided not to tell her guys until after Leopold finished his mid-term tests. So that was the day I told Henry. "We need another talk," I said. "Come on, sit down.

"I've decided where I'm going next year," I went on. "I'm going to Calgary."

He nodded. "Will you live with Janice?" he asked.

"Yes. She and I have decided to become partners. I want you to know that you can always count on me. On us. Anytime you want to live with me, you'll be welcome. You could finish high school there. Or go to university later. There'll always be a room for you if you want it."

"Nope," he said firmly, shaking his head. "I want to stay here where my friends are. I want to stay in my school. Will you visit? Can I come visit you?"

"Yes, of course. And we can be in touch as much as you like by phone."

"Mum ..."

"Yes?"

"I knew ... about you and Janice, I mean. When she was here in November. I mean, you were sleeping together."

"Yes," I said. "I thought you'd ask about it. Does this bother you?"

He began to cry. "I don't want you to take the cats," he said. "They're my girlie-girls. And I don't want you saying Anatol and Leopold are like sons to you. You have two sons — me and Hugo. Not them."

I hugged him and felt the familiar exchange of love. "Don't worry," I said. "You can keep the cats here. I know you'll look after them well. I'll take them if you ever want me to. And no one can replace you and Hugo in my heart. Bea, either. I love you."

"I love you too, Mum."

That night I called Hugo.

"No problem," he said. "I mean, I'm not homophobic or anything. But I don't especially like Janice. Where will you be living?" I told him, and explained about Henry.

"What do you dislike about Janice?" I asked.

"Don't know. I just trust my gut feeling on people."

"That's okay," I said. "I hope in time you'll change your mind. If not, it won't make a difference between you and me. I'll always love you and want to see you."

There was silence.

"Mum?"

"Yeah."

"I'm worried that if you're not dressing for men any more you'll lose your looks."

Bea took it better. "Wow, Mum," she giggled after I'd finished my long-distance explanation. "And now for something *completely* different!" She laughed. "I think it's *great*! Peter and I are musicians, so — trust me — we're used to gay people. Like, *lots* of gay people. But I haven't even *met* Janice. I want to meet her as soon as possible."

"Well, sweetie, that won't be for a while, unless you're planning a trip."

"Not until next March, probably," she said.

"Well, I'll send pictures. Meanwhile, I'm so glad you're not upset. Your acceptance of this means so much to me. What you say makes me feel really, really happy."

I felt dazed. Almost too dazed to get onto e-mail to see how Janice's guys were taking it.

"We had a family pow-wow," the message said.

David and I — actually David — told the guys what was happening. We started by telling them we were getting divorced. They were surprised, and immediately came up with lots of ideas about how we could stay together. We just listened for a while before telling them, no, this is final. We told them they could choose whether to stay on at the house or live with us. Told them they'd have lots of time to decide. D. and I want them to see that we are friends. That over the next couple of months until I move out there are no fights or conflicts. That there are civilized ways of splitting up.

Then we got onto JE. How you and I would be living together, but that we'd still be seeing David and them. We'd be here in Calgary where they could visit and see me whenever they wanted. There was all this discussion. Leopold said, "But it's every man's God-given right to have a woman." Then he caught himself and said, "Oh my God, what am I saying." They wanted to know where we'd be living. I had to tell them we didn't know, but we'd try to find a place not too far away.

Finally, the penny dropped for Anatol, who, after all, is only twelve. Finally he looked around at us all and said, "You mean ... my mother is *gay*?"

Look, I think you'll like this townhouse. I took A. over with me to look again, and he loved it. The agent says it hasn't sold because the spaces are so quirky. I can't really describe. I hope it hasn't sold by the time you get here. I love it BECAUSE the spaces are so quirky. And the light is phenomenal. Gorgeous. The bedroom has a south AND a west window. Big elm tree outside. Bonus: it's only five blocks from D. and the guys. I'm so HAPPY. Can't wait to see you this time. Forever and ever, J.

Next were our parents. "I asked D. to tell them," she e-mailed.

We went over there today. They were fairly upset. Father went into his minister role giving us advice. I had to shut him down. Mother wanted to blame me, since she's convinced women cause all the trouble in the world. They both think this, actually. We didn't tell them about JE.

One thing at a time. We just told them about separating.
They like D. What I told them was that I expect them to
continue to treat D. as one of the family, just as they
always have. We explained that there were no fights. No
conflicts. We would have no problem attending family
events together. They were mystified, but relieved not to
have to make choices, I think.

I drove to Barrie to tell mine. I decided to tell them separately.
First my mother.
"Mum," I said. "I have something really important to tell you.
Janice and I have decided to live together."
"Well, that will be nice," she said. "What about her husband?"
"They are getting divorced. Amicably."
"Well, it does make sense economically, I guess. And I hate to
see you so lonely. I've been dreading your bringing another man
home."
"Mum, I don't just mean sharing a house, sharing expenses. I
mean ..."
"You mean you intend to live as a couple?"
"Yes."
"Well, don't tell your father. I can understand it. Though I
won't tell my friends. I couldn't tell them. But don't tell your
father. He's dreadfully opposed to homosexuality."
"I can't promise that, Mum. I want him to know."
Later I tackled my father. "Dad, I want to tell you something
important."
He looked up from his ongoing game of solitaire quizzically.
He was eighty-three and his memory was a bit unreliable.
"Do you remember Janice?"
"Yes. She's that nice dark girl. The lawyer, isn't she?"

"Yep. She and I have decided to live together."

"Live together? Seems sensible. Good."

Just then my mother walked in. "Yes," she said. "Donald ... they've ... made a commitment to each other. To live together."

He looked at me. He understood. It was all right.

"It's drink time, isn't it?" he said looking at the clock. It was early, but for once he'd break his rule: No drinks until the sun is over the yardarm. "I'd better get the single malt out." And he made his way into the dining room and emerged with his precious single-malt scotch.

Next were Janice's brothers and my sisters. Each of us got the warmest response from the much younger siblings we'd helped raise. My younger sister was enthusiastic. "I felt there was something between you two when I met Janice. Great! She's very good for you. She seems like a soulmate." Janice's youngest brother simply said, "No problem here. Wendy and I will have you both over as soon as we can."

Our other siblings said nothing much at all.

Finally came our friends. We didn't want anyone we cared for to hear via the gossip we knew would race through the academic world. We *wanted* the gossip, wanted it to inform acquaintances and colleagues, but we wanted to tell our close friends in person first. That meant telling them as simultaneously as possible.

I invited each of mine to lunch on consecutive days. And almost every one said, "I'm not surprised." I was bewildered. *I* was surprised, very surprised. Why weren't they? Members of my women's group said they had picked up on the vibes between Janice and me the evening I took her to meet them. That group had fostered one partnership between two women who claimed they knew, had been certain, just seeing us together. They welcomed me into the sisterhood and eagerly extolled the joys of lesbian life.

Gail and her husband, who had helped me so much through all the pain of separating from Paul, said they knew how close Janice and I had become. They weren't surprised because they couldn't see how I could trust a man after Paul.

Another friend — much younger — said she wasn't surprised because she knew how much more intimate women friends can be than a man and a woman. She couldn't fathom the sex, but she could certainly see how sharing life with a woman might be wonderful. Before long she was speculating on who among her girlfriends she could imagine choosing.

The American lesbian couple Paul and I had known for years — a doctor and a writer/professor — travelled up to see me on their annual visit. I warned them I had something important to tell them. They sat in my kitchen while I explained. "See," Anita said. "I was right. I told you this would be what she had to tell us."

"How could you know?" I asked. "I never envied you as a couple. Never wondered about whether life with a woman would suit me."

"I always thought you could be a sister. Don't know why. Just did. I'm not surprised," said Anita.

"But you could knock me over with the proverbial feather," said Beth. And they both gave me big hugs.

There was one couple I could not pin down to a specific lunch date. Eventually, after I'd persisted without success, they asked me over to their place for dinner instead.

While Jack got martinis, Cindy asked me impatiently, "What *is* it? Have you met someone? Don't tell me you're getting married again."

"Well," I said, deciding to join in the twenty-questions spirit, "sort of."

"Sort of? What do you mean? Who is he? Is it someone I know?"

"Yes, you've met." I remembered bringing Janice along to their big annual garden party the previous fall.

"Not that historian." She named a colleague.

"No."

"Thank God! He'd be real trouble. Who *is* he?"

"It's not a he. It's a she."

Cindy was speechless for a moment. Her eyes widened. "A *she*? Who?"

"Janice Dickin McGinnis. I brought her to your party last fall, don't you remember?"

"Vaguely. A dark woman, interesting. Yes ... yes. I do. Wasn't she married?"

"Not now."

Cindy thought for a moment. Then she said, "Look, Elspeth. Are you sure this isn't some sort of intellectual experiment? Virginia Woolf ... that sort of thing? Lots of writers try this sort of thing out just to find out what it's like."

"No," I said quietly. "I love her."

"Jack will have a fit. He's put you on a pedestal for years. He thinks you're the quintessential blonde.

"Well!" she said, as Jack brought a tray of martinis into the room. "Jack, Elspeth has some *very* interesting news for you."

"She's not getting married again, is she?" he said in his urbane way.

"Sort of."

Jack perked up. He raised a sardonic eyebrow. "Who's the lucky guy? Anyone I know?"

"You've met," I said.

"Is it someone in academe?" Jack was my colleague at U of T.

"Yes."

"Social sciences?"

"Yes."

He looked to Cindy. She sat beaming, but didn't give him a clue.

"It's not ... what's-his-name."

"Nope," we said in stereo.

He smiled in the knowing way he had when he made jokes. "It's a woman, I suppose."

"Yes," we said, again in stereo.

He chuckled and went right on. "So is he one of our colleagues, Elspeth? Who's the lucky bugger?"

"Jack, Jack," said Cindy, "didn't you hear us? It *is* a woman. It's Janice ... what's her last name, Elspeth?"

"Dickin McGinnis."

"Janice Dickin McGinnis. Elspeth brought her to our party last fall. Remember? Interesting woman." Jack just sat there. He was white, crumpled somehow.

"So, where will you live?" Cindy went on. She was full of questions. How had we met. How had this happened. What was the sex like. Jack said nothing.

Eventually we all moved into the dining room. Jack was still silent. His colour had changed from white to grey. When Cindy got up to clear the table for dessert, Jack quietly left the room and went upstairs. Cindy called him when she had dessert ready, and he slowly descended the stairs wearing his pyjamas and dressing gown. He looked ill.

"Well, I can take a hint. I guess this means it's time to go," I joked to Cindy. I finished my dessert quickly, accepted a quick, warm hug from Cindy and drove home.

I never heard again from all those York couples I had entertained with Paul for fifteen years. All those parties. All that care taken not to intimidate the wives, not to flirt with the husbands. All those picnics, visits, chats about children. Gone. It would be a year before I stopped feeling that loss.

Janice lost two couples she'd been close to for twenty years. One told her what she was doing was wrong. The other never replied to her repeated invitations for lunch or coffee. A woman she described as her oldest friend also evaporated. But her other friends responded with good wishes and requests to meet me as soon as we got settled. Some colleagues avoided her. Most — especially those in women's studies — congratulated her.

THE TOWNHOUSE WAS still for sale when I returned to Calgary. I fell in love with it at once. It was the corner house of an eleven-unit complex around a European courtyard garden. Each white unit had a different-coloured door. Ours was blue. The effect was that of a Mondrian painting. "Connaught Gardens," as it was called, after the Duke of Connaught who had visited Calgary more than once early this century, had won awards for its architect and designer. It would be by far the nicest place I had ever lived in. The price had dropped to within our range, and David came through with the financing we needed to buy it. In a matter of days "Blue Doors" was ours. We would take possession 30 June, right after our month and a half in the lighthouse on the coast of P.E.I. Our honeymoon.

I was happy with a happiness I'd never felt before. I felt more real than I'd ever felt before. My hair was slowly returning to its natural colour — dark ash with streaks of grey.

Our life together began exactly four years from the day we

met in Edinburgh. On the fourth of May, I met Janice at the Toronto airport, as I had done so many times before.

We clasped each other tight, saying nothing. Finally, she said, "Darling."

"Yes," I replied.

And we exchanged anniversary gifts as we had each year on the fourth of May. For her, my Aunt Winnie's 1921 diamond watch. "I loved seeing this on her small wrist. Now I can admire it on yours," I said.

And for me a Swiss Army knife for our hikes.

"No dyke should be without one," she said, laughing, and took me in her arms.